Cambridge Topics in Geography

Editors   Alan R.H. Baker, Emmanuel College, Cambridge
Colin Evans, King's College, Wimbledon

Slopes and Weathering

M.J. Clark & R.J. Small
Department of Geography, University of Southampton

*The right of the
University of Cambridge
to print and sell
all manner of books
was granted by
Henry VIII in 1534.
The University has printed
and published continuously*

Cambridge University Press

Cambridge
New York   Port Chester
Melbourne   Sydney

Published by the Press Syndicate of the University of Cambridge
The Pitt Building, Trumpington Street, Cambridge CB2 1RP
40 West 20th Street, New York, NY 10011, USA
10 Stamford Road, Oakleigh, Melbourne 3166, Australia

First published 1982
Fourth printing 1990

Printed in Great Britain at the University Press, Cambridge

Library of Congress catalogue card number: 81–18025

British Library Cataloguing in Publication Data

Small, R. J.
Slopes and weathering.–(Cambridge topics
in geography. 2nd series)
1. Slopes (Physical geography)
I. Title.   II. Clark, M. J.
551.4´36   GB448

ISBN 0 521 23340 2 hard covers

ISBN 0 521 29926 8 paperback

Maps and diagrams by Parkway Illustrated Press

Contents

Preface

The study of slopes has long tended to be regarded by many students as a dose of medicine - grudgingly acknowledged to be 'doing them good', but to be taken only in small portions and only when absolutely necessary. It is easy to see why this should be so: study becomes much simpler when its subject is a clearly defined feature that can be investigated or described with some precision. Slopes fail to meet this standard because they extend largely unbroken across the whole land surface, so that it is rare to be able to put a line around a slope feature to study it or draw it. For this reason, slopes have earned the reputation of being difficult both to research and to conceptualise compared with many branches of the subject. Whilst river systems have been studied fruitfully within the boundaries conveniently provided by the drainage basin or catchment, the less well defined slope system has lapsed into neglect at introductory level. Even at a research level, investigations have until recently often been directed at fragments of slopes (individual features, processes or relationships) rather than attempting to master the system as a whole. Another handicap has been the extremely slow rate at which slope processes act and slope forms change, which has made study difficult compared with the relative dynamism of river channels or coasts.

In this book we have attempted to show slopes in a more favourable light, seeing their study as a challenge rather than a chore. So much of the 'scenery' around us is made up of slopes, and so much of the mystery of landforms is locked up in the development of slopes, that to ignore this most fundamental of topics is tantamount to abandoning the struggle to understand the landscape before it has even begun. We are not alone in finding fascination in slope study. Generations of geologists, geomorphologists, hydrologists and engineers have produced between them a staggering amount of literature. Much of this has rightly faded into oblivion, but some has survived relatively unscathed for a century or more. The chapters that follow endeavour to recognise these historical roots of the subject, and to trace their growth into the ideas that receive emphasis today, thus demonstrating that our present interests are simply a point that has been reached in a continuing story of academic and practical development. There are few questions in slope study on which the last word has been written.

In keeping with this recognition of the changing priorities of the subject, we have steered a middle course between the traditional focus on form and the more recent concern with process and material. Some topics, such as the engineer's stability analysis or the quantitative geomorphologist's interest in numerical slope modelling, receive only passing mention - not because they lack importance, but because we feel that other aspects should take precedence in an introductory text. For some students with a general interest in landscape this admittedly brief and partial survey may be sufficient in itself. For others it may awaken an interest that can be pursued in more specialist texts. We hope that for all it will help to dispel any lingering feeling that slope study is a medicine to be avoided.

John Small, Michael Clark, *University of Southampton*

1 The slope problem

Slopes are the most basic of all landforms, and for that reason alone command the attention of physical geographers. Additionally, slopes directly affect many of man's activities – agriculture, road and railway construction, house building, land drainage, and so on – and, where associated with various kinds of instability, can actually pose a serious threat to man. Understanding the mechanisms of slope development therefore constitutes a vital task for the applied geomorphologist. It is, however, by no means an easy task. Many slopes appear to be extremely simple in form, and seem to pose no obvious problems of development. Often there is little evidence, apart from slight soil movement, that the slopes are actually undergoing change. Yet the more slopes are studied, the more they are seen to be highly complex landforms. They not only vary greatly from one locality to another in steepness and degree of active development, reflecting the influences of weathering (Chapter 2), transport processes (Chapter 3), rock type (Chapter 6) and climate (Chapter 7), but display subtleties of form that require very careful analysis (Chapter 4). For a true understanding of slopes the evidence from many areas needs to be assembled, with the aim of constructing general theories of slope evolution (Chapter 5).

Some problems of slope study

1 *Rate of development*

Slopes in highly resistant rocks, or in climates where weathering and transport are inactive, experience very slow rates of change. Many slopes 'retreat' by less than 1 mm per year, so that within the life-span of an observer they are virtually 'static' landforms. Yet to explain slope evolution geomorphologists need information as to whether slopes are becoming steeper, undergoing parallel retreat or declining, whether they are changing from convex to concave in profile, and so on. Without reliable data they have to hypothesise on the basis of assumptions rather than real evidence.

2 *The legacy of the past*

Slopes, like other landforms, may be inherited largely from past conditions, or in other words they are 'relict' features. Over much of the world present-day climatic conditions, and related processes, have existed for 10,000 years or less. Often climatic change since the last glacial period of the Pleistocene has resulted in the replacement of active slope processes by ineffective processes, as in the hyper-arid deserts where weathering and erosion may now be virtually non-existent. In southern Britain, which experienced periglacial conditions during the Pleistocene, present-day processes have only slightly modified the relict slope forms. For example, solution on the chalk has produced a surface lowering of slopes by a mere 1 m during the Post-glacial period, so that features produced by past gelifraction and gelifluction remain almost intact. Real difficulties of interpretation arise when the imprint of past and present slope-forming processes is preserved in more equal measure.

3 *Measurement of slope processes*

Even where slopes are being actively modified, measurements of the processes responsible are often difficult to make. For example, in absolute terms mass transport is extremely slow (1–2 mm per year in temperate climates); moreover, the actual measurement may involve the digging of pits which can disturb the natural process and give misleading results. Again, surface 'erosion' by rainwash – an intermittent process – can be measured by pins inserted into the soil surface, but patience and great precision are required since the lowering of the ground surface by this agent may be considerably less than 0.1 mm per year under temperate conditions.

4 *The multivariate nature of slopes*

A particularly difficult problem of slope study stems from the fact that many factors (climatic, geological, hydrological, pedological and vegetational) and many processes (varied types of weathering and several modes of transport) interact in the formation of slopes. In the simplest terms slopes can be regarded as the outcome of 'active' processes shaping 'passive' materials, with form depending on the time during which the processes have operated. In other words, slopes can be analysed in terms of *structure, process and stage*, as outlined by W. M. Davis (1899). A more realistic approach, and one increasingly adopted, is to view the slope as a *natural system*, within which there are numerous and complex 'linkages' between factors, processes and forms.

Fig. 1.1 The slope system, in relation to a convexo-rectilinear-concave slope.

The slope system

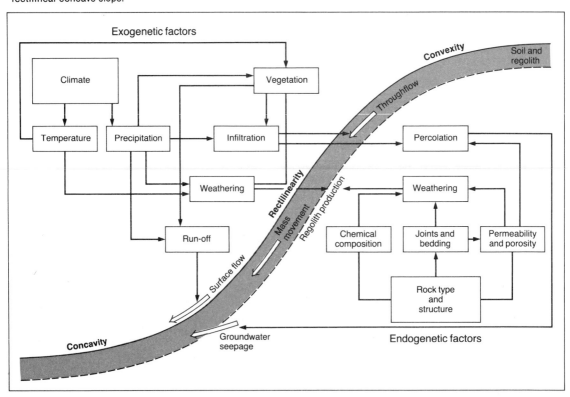

Chorley and Kennedy (1971) identify three types of functional system: *isolated*, *closed* and *open*. Of these, open systems occur widely in geomorphology; their prime attribute is that they exchange energy and mass with their surroundings. For instance, a slope receives *inputs of energy* (from solar radiation, falling raindrops, wind). Moreover, the very existence of the slope (with its difference of height between crest and base) means that it possesses a 'store' of potential energy which is converted into kinetic energy by way of rainwash and mass movements. The slope also receives *inputs of mass*, in the form of water from rainfall, snow-melt, springs and seepages, inorganic minerals from the weathering of bedrock, organic material from vegetation, and so on.

Just as it gains energy and mass, so the slope system loses energy and mass. The principal *output of energy* is loss of heat (for example, by nocturnal radiation or by heat friction generated within the mobile regolith). *Outputs of mass* include water, weathered debris, solutes and organic waste, all of which most frequently leave the system by way of streams or other transporting media at the slope base.

This leads us to emphasise that the slope system cannot be studied in total isolation, since there are fundamental links with other natural systems. For example, the atmospheric system directly influences inputs of both energy and mass (solar radiation and precipitation) into the slope system. Modification of the atmospheric system, as long-term climatic changes occur, necessarily requires some readjustment of the slope system. Again, it is unrealistic to dissociate the slope and fluvial systems. Erosion by streams may cause steepening of slopes, by downcutting or lateral undercutting. The result will be accelerated evacuation of debris from the slope (affecting the rate of slope recession); at the same time, the debris entering the stream may influence the form and steepness of the channel, and help to determine whether the valley floor is incised or aggraded.

Slope systems are sustained by inputs of energy and mass, which may be balanced by outputs, giving a *steady state* or *equilibrium* condition. At first sight this might seem unlikely, on the grounds that short-term changes of weather and climate might produce irregular rates of weathering and spasmodic transport of slope debris, that will not be exactly matched by transfer of material into the stream at the slope foot. It is, in fact, safest to regard equilibrium as an average condition, obtaining over a number of years. More problematic are the longer-term changes (climatic oscillations in the Pleistocene, varied rates of land uplift, positive and negative movements of base level). These will initiate modifications of the slope system; and since in some areas and/or at some times such changes are both continuously operative and rapid, equilibrium – even as an average condition – may not be easily achieved. On the other hand, there are areas (usually underlain by weak rocks, and subjected to rapid weathering and transport processes) where equilibrium can be established and maintained relatively easily.

Where the factors controlling slopes undergo change, resulting in increased or decreased inputs and outputs, the slope system will necessarily adjust to the new conditions. A simple hypothetical example will illustrate the manner of this adjustment. A change in climate from humid (with ample and well distributed rainfall) to semi-arid (with reduced, spasmodic and sometimes intense rainfall) will lead to a reduction in vegetation cover on the slope. The efficiency of running water as a transporting agent will thereby be increased dramatically, and the regolith will be stripped away, especially

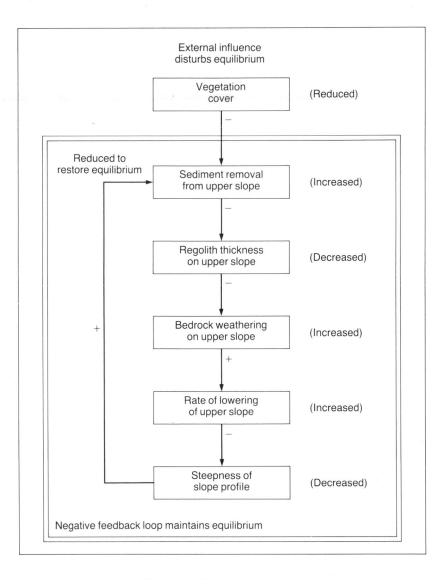

Fig. 1.2 Maintenance of equilibrium within the slope system.

External influence disturbs equilibrium

Vegetation cover   (Reduced)

Reduced to restore equilibrium

Sediment removal from upper slope   (Increased)

Regolith thickness on upper slope   (Decreased)

Bedrock weathering on upper slope   (Increased)

Rate of lowering of upper slope   (Increased)

Steepness of slope profile   (Decreased)

Negative feedback loop maintains equilibrium

from the upper part of the slope. The bare rock here will then be more rapidly weathered, leading to a reduction in overall slope angle; in other words the slope will have begun to 'adjust its geometry' or more simply change form. The key to the self-regulation of slope systems, so that they move towards a restoration of equilibrium between inputs and outputs, is the mechanism known as *negative feedback*. In this, an external change produces a series of reactions within the system which offset the effects of the original change (Fig. 1.2). In the example discussed, the external change increases the efficiency of surface wash; however, this then leads to a reduction of slope gradient, which in turn reduces again the velocity and power of the surface wash.

The existence of equilibrium within the slope system is demonstrated by two lines of evidence. First, if the soil/regolith layer over the slope as a whole is relatively shallow and of approximately even thickness, a balance between the production of waste by weathering and its removal by mass movements and running water is indicated. Absence of such a layer shows that transport is 'over-effective' compared with weathering (as on a steep bare-rock face), and such slopes are therefore known as 'weathering-limited', since their rate of development is constrained mainly by the rate of weathering. On the other hand, if the layer is built up to a considerable thickness, transport must be relatively 'under-effective', and these slopes are known as 'transport-limited' in their development. Secondly, it is logical to expect that transport processes which are exactly capable of removing soil and regolith at a rate equal to production will themselves be related to a particular slope angle (or have a particular *morphological* expression). Field and map measurements have in fact shown that within small areas of uniform climate, relief, rock type and drainage density, *equilibrium slope angles* do occur. These angles are diagnosed from the occurrence of maximum slope angles (derived from a sufficiently large sample of slope profiles) which show little deviation from the mean maximum slope angle for the area concerned (Strahler 1950). The equilibrium angle itself is, of course, that which promotes a rate of transport just sufficient to remove debris as rapidly as it is produced.

Slopes and man

Much early study of slopes fell into the category of 'pure geomorphology' (that is, slope forms and processes were studied for their own intrinsic interest, rather than for their relevance to man and his activities). However, the practical aspects of slope geomorphology are being increasingly appreciated (Chapter 8). Slopes can affect man profoundly; and man, in turn, can cause important modifications to slope systems.

Slope steepness particularly affects man's activities in areas of high relief, where slopes are often too precipitous for cultivation or habitation, and soils are so thin that they have to be gathered into artificial terraces. Steep slopes can give rise to serious hazards, such as landslides of various kinds which can destroy villages, farms and cropland and sometimes cause immense loss of life. Landslides occur in areas of potential and actual slope instability, which is caused by *increases in shear stress* and/or *decreases in shear strength* of the slope-forming materials (Cooke and Doornkamp 1974). Increases in shear stress are the result of several causes: removal of support for the slope, owing to basal undercutting by rivers, glaciers and waves; disturbing processes such as the accumulation of weathering debris at certain points on the slope; transitory shocks produced by earthquakes; and the build-up of high internal pore-pressures where water collects within the regolith or underlying rock. Decreases in shear strength also take several forms: reduced strength of slope materials (for example, by the formation of pressure-release joints on the walls of glacial troughs); reduced cohesion of regoliths owing to advanced weathering; and reduced internal friction associated with high pore-water pressures. It is a vital task of applied geomorphology to identify the sites of potential slope instability, and to suggest remedial action (since a major 'trigger mechanism' is the accumulation of groundwater, drainage of the slope and diversion of surface-water flows from above it are often effective measures).

Man can himself modify the 'natural' slope system in a variety of ways. He can play a significant role in initiating or reactivating landslides, for example by excavations, building construction, formation of tip-heaps, and dam building, all of which can promote instability by (i) loading the slope, (ii) removing vital support, and (iii) increasing pore-water pressures. Conversely, he can counter instability by 'grading' slopes at the natural angle of repose, by drainage (see above), and by the construction of retaining structures. Problems sometimes occur when man unwittingly revives dormant landslides, as in areas

Erosion of sandy soils following cultivation: southern England.

of past periglaciation where solifluction lobes have dried out and become vegetated. When the 'toes' of such slides are removed (for instance, by road cuttings) movement may recur. In present-day periglacial areas, disturbance of permafrost can have alarming consequences. French (1975) describes how the stripping of surface gravels for airstrip construction at Sachs Harbour, Banks Island, Canada, has resulted in rapid thermokarst development. With melting of the permafrost table the ground surface has subsided, and has been transformed into innumerable small mounds and linear depressions. In summer standing water becomes abundant, and the whole area impassable. When this sort of activity takes place on slopes, such man-induced thermokarst causes rapid mudflows and deep gullying.

The most widespread impact of man on the slope system occurs where vegetation is removed for arable cultivation or by overgrazing. The result is 'accelerated erosion' (by contrast with the 'geological erosion' of undisturbed slopes). Processes such as soil creep are comparatively unaffected, but the action of running water may be enormously increased. The most severe effects are from 'raindrop erosion', whereby soil particles are detached by the impact of the drop and redistributed by the splash effect (with a net movement down slope). The particles thus disturbed are then readily transported by surface run-off, which without the aid of rainsplash would be relatively ineffective. One example of accelerated erosion is provided by an area of silt-loams in the U.S.A. During a 10-year period losses of soil in tonnes per acre were recorded as follows: for areas of continuous maize cropping (with strips of bare earth between rows) 39–53 tonnes; for areas of rotated crops of maize, oats and clover 5–18 tonnes; and for areas of lucerne and blue grass less than 0.1 tonnes.

A case study of slope form and evolution: the New Forest, Hampshire

Even at this introductory stage it is useful to undertake a simple case study, designed to illustrate the scope of slope study at a local scale.

1 *Relief and geology*

The New Forest is an area of subdued relief. Maximum height above sea-level is 127 m; and the broad valleys of the northern Forest, where dissection is greatest, rarely have a depth in excess of 50 m. The area is underlain by Tertiary sands and clays, which are capped extensively by sub-angular flint gravels (Plateau Gravels) of 1–6 m in thickness. The gravels are more restricted and discontinuous in the north, where they occur mainly as narrow interfluve cappings; in the south they form broad heathland plateaus, separating narrow valleys.

2 *Slope forms* (Fig. 1.3)

Field survey by Lewin (1966) has shown that slope profiles in the New Forest vary considerably in detail, depending on valley dimensions and other factors. However, in terms of overall form most slopes are convexo-rectilinear-concave (Fig. 1.1). Of the three components the rectilinear segment is the least important, usually occupying less than 10% of the total slope length. The summital convexity (present on all slopes surveyed) occupies 30–60% of individual slope profiles, and the basal concavity 20–60%. Owing to the incoherent nature of the sands and the susceptibility of the clays to mass slumping, slope angles are mainly gentle. Mean slope angles are from $2°$ to $10°$ (falling mainly in the range $5°$–$8°$); maximum slope angles are usually between $9°$ and $17°$, with a distinct 'peak' at $12°$–$13°$. Very few slopes exceed $20°$; if they do they are normally unstable, showing that the maximum repose angle is about $20°$ (and this is usually developed on gravel-capped slopes). Oversteepening is well illustrated in the active marine cliffs on the southern margins of the New Forest, along the margins of Christchurch Bay. In detail, many New Forest slopes are of complex form, and comprise sequences of convexities and concavities resulting from geological influences and the intermittent downcutting of the Forest streams.

3 *Processes of slope formation*

As in other parts of Southern England slopes in the New Forest are to a large extent relict features. The valleys are partly the result of incision by meltwater streams during the Pleistocene; solifluction deposits (comprising a mixture of sand, clay and gravel) mantle the lower slopes; and the steeper upper slopes are indented by shallow depressions ('dells') marking zones of concentrated periglacial 'erosion' – some are, perhaps, miniature nivation hollows. There are other indications of more active past processes in the form of 'seepage

Fig. 1.3 Selected slopes in the New Forest, showing different profiles (after J. Lewin 1966).

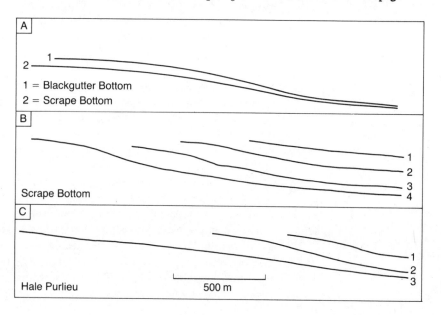

A

2 ——— 1 ———
1 = Blackgutter Bottom
2 = Scrape Bottom

B
—— 1
—— 2
—— 3
—— 4
Scrape Bottom

C
—— 1
—— 2
—— 3
Hale Purlieu   500 m

Fig. 1.4 Seepage steps in profile (A) and plan (B) (after C. G. Tuckfield 1973).

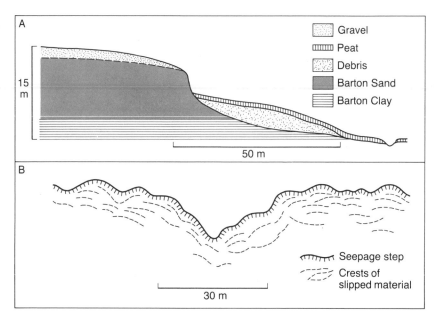

Valley-side slope in the New Forest.

steps' (Fig. 1.4), which are well developed in the central and northern parts of the Forest (Tuckfield 1973). These are 'linear' breaks of slope, penetrating main and subsidiary valleys. In profile there is usually a convex element above the step (which may itself comprise a near-vertical face), and a convex lobe of recently deposited debris below it. The steps broadly coincide with the junction of the permeable Barton Sand (above) and impermeable Barton Clay (below), which produces a zone of concentrated seepage even under present-day conditions. However, although the seepage steps are locally active, for the most part they appear to be stable. Presumably they were developed mainly during the Pleistocene, at times when extensive snow-melt in association with discontinuous permafrost fed large quantities of water into the permeable sands. At the same times intense spring sapping may have helped to drive back the steep margins of the gravels, especially where these rest on clays impeding downward drainage and giving rise to 'perched' water-tables.

On the clay slopes of the Forest (especially those of its steep northern margins) rotational landslips were also common under past periglacial conditions. On slopes in excess of 13° successive slips produced irregular profiles, with small 'scarplets' (at 20°–30°) at the rear of each individual slip (Tuckfield 1968).

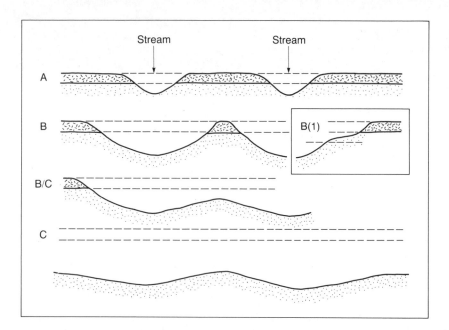

Fig. 1.5 Slope evolution in the New Forest (after J. Lewin 1966). Slopes are developing on a capping of Plateau Gravels (heavy shading) which overlies Tertiary sands and clays. Stages A and B develop through back-wearing, while C is a product of down-wasting or decline.

At the present time the New Forest slopes are locally modified by seepage, soil creep and, along tracks or where natural vegetation has been destroyed, quite powerful gullying. However, these processes have done little to destroy the periglacial slope features.

4 *Slope evolution*

Lewin (1966) has identified three main 'types' of slope development in the New Forest: (i) Slopes formed wholly within the Plateau Gravels (these are rare, and are mainly confined to the recently formed valleys in the southern New Forest). (ii) Slopes capped by Plateau Gravels, but 'eroded' mainly across Tertiary sands and clays (these are found mainly in the central and northern New Forest, within valleys that are older than those of the south). (iii) Slopes developed wholly on Tertiary sands and clays (former gravel cappings may have been removed from the crests of these slopes).

These three types may conveniently be viewed as successive 'stages' of slope evolution, as depicted in Fig. 1.5. In the formation of slope profiles of types (i) and (ii), steep segments of up to 20° have been maintained by a form of *back-wearing* or *parallel retreat*. In Fig. 1.5A the type (i) slopes have already been modified as the valley floor has cut through the capping of Plateau Gravel, and by the stage depicted in Fig. 1.5B slope retreat has produced a type (ii) profile. Slopes of type (iii) have undergone *wasting* or *decline*, as shown in Fig. 1.5C (the intermediate stage being Fig. 1.5B/C). Of course, this developmental sequence represents in some ways an over-simplification. The evolution of slopes of types (ii) and (iii) can be rendered more complex than is here suggested, either by episodes of stream downcutting (causing valley-side benches and terraces) or by the formation of seepage steps (involving back-wearing of lower parts of the slope at suitable lithological junctions), thus giving a stepped profile as shown in Fig. 1.5B(1). Nevertheless, the 'model' of evolution affords an introductory framework for the study of slopes in the New Forest, and indicates the way in which detailed investigations can lead to an improved understanding of slopes, and indeed of the landscape as a whole.

2 Weathering processes

Weathering has been defined in simple terms as the disintegration or decay of rocks *in situ*, or in more complex terms as 'the breakdown and alteration of materials near the earth's surface to products that are more in equilibrium with newly imposed physico-chemical conditions' (Ollier 1969). Weathering inevitably causes some displacement of the resultant debris, if only because changes of volume (crystal growth, swelling, leaching, eluviation of fines) accompany individual processes. However, where substantial movement of weathered detritus occurs, as a result of gravity-controlled mechanisms such as soil creep, running water and rockfalls, this is referred to as transport (Chapter 3).

For purposes of convenience many authorities recognise two main types of weathering: *physical weathering*, which is the breakdown of the rock into fragments by entirely mechanical methods, and *chemical weathering*, which involves the decomposition of rock minerals by agents such as water, oxygen, carbon dioxide and organic acids. A separate category of *biotic weathering* is also sometimes identified; however, this involves both physical processes (such as the splitting of rocks by tree roots) and chemical processes (such as the rotting of limestone by bird droppings) and is therefore arguably embraced by the two main types of weathering.

In reality the distinction between physical and chemical weathering is somewhat arbitrary; in most situations they not only act together, but can reinforce each other. Where a rock is cracked by a purely physical mechanism access is provided for rainwater which can chemically alter minerals along the margins of the crack. This is likely even in areas (such as high mountains) where physical processes such as frost splitting are assumed to be dominant. Conversely a rock that is subjected to chemical decay will have its void spaces enlarged owing to the removal of solutes. This will allow the entry of larger amounts of water, and if freezing occurs ice crystals will form and, by exerting considerable stress (p. 16), will encourage granular disaggregation. Again, chemical processes can have a mainly physical expression, as in hydration or salt crystallisation in cracks just beneath the rock surface. This may result in the breaking away of plate-like rock fragments (spalls) or small-scale exfoliation. Many important processes take place at the microscopic scale, where physical and chemical activity are particularly difficult to separate.

Factors in rock weathering

Weathering processes are influenced by *endogenetic* and *exogenetic* factors. Endogenetic factors are related to the structure and composition of the rock itself. The presence of rock minerals susceptible to particular chemical processes (for example, calcite which is affected by carbonation and feldspars which are altered by hydrolysis) will influence the pattern and effectiveness of chemical weathering. Rock texture will also be important. Fine-grained rocks, which possess a close and intricate network of crystal boundaries, may weather more rapidly than coarse-grained rocks, in which there are fewer lines of weakness. The occurrence of joints and bedding planes, together with minute cracks or 'micro-fissures', is a vital factor, for these act as strong foci for various weathering processes. Rocks which possess few joints ('massive' rocks) are usually very resistant to weathering, and frequently form bold free faces and tor-like landforms.

Exogenetic factors include climate and vegetation. Climate determines the availability of water, ambient atmospheric and soil temperatures, and ranges of temperature (annual and diurnal) within an area. Water is required for most – indeed possibly all – weathering processes, both physical and chemical. It is not surprising therefore that in deserts weathering is largely superficial, producing shallow mantles and soils, and acts selectively along structurally very weak zones or in shaded locations where some moisture can persist (Cooke and Warren 1973). Recession of rock faces in deserts may be as low as 0.5 mm per 10,000 years, by contrast with 1–2 mm per year in the Swiss Alps or Brazil. High temperatures also influence weathering processes, as is shown by Van't Hoff's rule which states that rates of chemical reactions rise 2 to 3 times for every $10\,°C$ increase in temperature. Since soil temperatures in the temperate and tropical zones differ by as much as $15–20\,°C$ it is likely that, on the grounds of this factor alone, tropical weathering rates will exceed those of temperate regions by up to 4 times (Thomas 1974). An additional factor in the humid tropics is the abundance of groundwater and decaying vegetal matter (which in rain forests is supplied at an annual rate of 100–200 tonnes per hectare, by comparison with the 20–25 tonnes of the cool temperate coniferous forest); the latter releases organic acids which aid some types of chemical decay. Weathering rates in the humid tropics may be up to 40 times those of temperate regions – a fact which helps to explain the formation of deep tropical regoliths. Temperature ranges are, as will be shown below, important controls over some types of physical weathering, notably frost splitting and granular disintegration by ground ice crystals.

Physical weathering processes

(a) **Pressure release**   This is not in the strict sense a process of weathering, but it is so intimately associated with the physical disintegration of rocks and may assist so many true weathering processes that it requires detailed consideration here. It is well known that a rock experiencing great confining pressure (for example, a granite or gneiss formed at depth within the earth's crust) will increase in strength. However, with reduction of this confining pressure (for example, by the exposure of the deep-seated rock owing to the denudation of overlying strata) strength will be decreased and the rock will undergo elastic expansion. Because rocks *in situ* are confined 'laterally', expansion must be at right angles to the ground surface, resulting in a series of cracks parallel to that surface. Such *sheet joints* have been widely observed in granitic rocks, where they constitute 'pseudo-bedding' planes; these, together with the normal vertical intersecting joints, frequently give rise to a 'cuboidal' joint structure. Alternatively the sheet joints may be dominant, as on dome-like inselbergs the margins of which comprise concentric shells of rock. The formation of pressure-release joints may actually cause rock disintegration – indeed 'rock bursting' has been observed in limestone quarries as well as in natural situations (for example, the uparching of sheets of gneiss beyond the snouts of retreating glaciers). However, in many instances the

Granite inselberg near Kaduna, Nigeria, showing massive sheet jointing.

joints form lines of weakness which can be penetrated by agents of physical and chemical weathering. In this way they are progressively 'opened up' to the point at which sliding or collapse of the joint-bounded blocks can occur.

The nature and age of sheet jointing varies greatly. Sometimes the joints form massive structures, with individual sheets measuring 5–10 m in thickness. However, joint spacing may decrease to a few centimetres near the ground

Fig. 2.1 Ancient (A) and more recent (B) sheet joints and their relationships with the land surface.

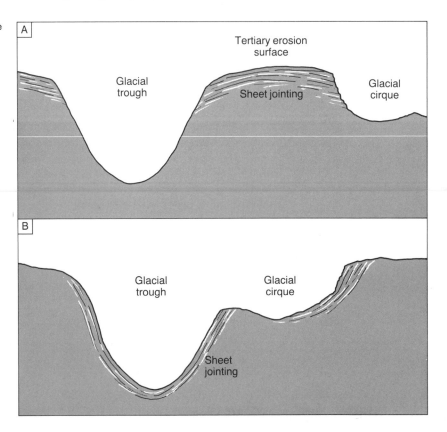

surface. It is likely that pressure release can also produce minor cracks and micro-fissures, which favour spalling and small-scale exfoliation. Some sheet joints are developed parallel to ancient land surfaces, as in the Cairngorms of Scotland (Fig. 2.1A). Here the joints 'mirror' the late-Tertiary erosion surfaces on summits and interfluves, but are 'transected' by more recently formed glacial cirques and troughs (Sugden 1968). In other areas the sheet jointing is more recent (Fig. 2.1B), and has developed parallel to valley-side slopes, the headwalls of cirques and the margins of deep glacial troughs (as in Norwegian fjords incised into Pre-Cambrian gneiss). Once in existence sheet joints of this type tend to perpetuate landforms (including valley-side and inselberg slopes) as successive layers of rock are detached from the surface and additional joints are developed by pressure release at depth.

(b) Frost weathering   This is the most widespread type of pure physical weathering. It is characteristic of high latitudes (as in present-day periglacial environments), of high altitudes (even in the equatorial zone), of mid-latitude regions in winter, and perhaps of some deserts. Cooke and Warren (1973) note that in the Mojave Desert, U.S.A., up to 100 'freezing days' occur each year, mainly during the season of greatest precipitation, when moisture for ground ice formation is most readily available. However, much of this desert lies at an altitude of 500–1,200 m; it is unlikely that frost weathering is of much significance over, say, most of the Sahara or Arabian Deserts.

A traditional view of frost weathering is that it results from 'frost wedging' or 'splitting', which occurs when water penetrates joints and bedding planes, undergoes a phase change from liquid to ice, and thus has the potential to expand by approximately 10% if unconfined by the rigidity of the surrounding rock. Successive frost cycles will widen fissures, and eventually permit large joint-bounded blocks to be detached. On a more modest scale frost weathering also affects rocks with micro-fissures and pores, within which ice crystals can develop, setting up large expansive stresses that can break the rock into relatively small clasts (flakes, aggregates of minerals and individual constituent grains). However, experiments indicate that frost processes do not produce very fine particles (of less than 0.6 mm in diameter). Thus where silt and clay particles are found in periglacial environments these are likely to have resulted from chemical weathering or abrasion.

The potential power of frost weathering is shown by the fact that theoretically freezing water in a totally confined cavity can exert a maximum pressure of 2,100 kg/cm^2 at $-22\,^\circ$C (below $-22\,^\circ$C the ice contracts, reducing stress). In nature such a force is not attained, for various reasons, not the least of which is that the rock will fracture long before maximum pressure is exerted. The average frost shattering force has been estimated as 14 kg/cm^2; even the strongest rocks can, if jointed, be split by a force of 100 kg/cm^2. Since conditions favouring frost wedging are achieved far less commonly than was once believed, it may be that cracking of rock due to shrinkage at low temperature, plus the influence of micro-chemical activity and the growth of individual ice crystals should be accorded much greater emphasis.

Frost action, working in conjunction with pressure release and other processes, is responsible for the recession of free faces, the accumulation beneath such faces of large masses of angular scree, and the development of block-fields and felsenmeer in present-day Arctic and high-mountain regions. However, these features seem sometimes to be the product of past rather

Frost weathering of a gritstone scarp: southern Pennines.

than contemporary activity. French (1976) suggests that many aspects of frost action in periglacial environments remain to be elucidated. One question concerns the relative importance of *annual* and *short-term frost cycles* (the latter lasting from one to four days and occurring mainly at the intermediate seasons). It has been widely assumed that *diurnal frost cycles* are, because of their high frequency of occurrence, the main causes of frost weathering. However, Chambers (1966) has shown that in an oceanic periglacial climate (Signy Island, Antarctica) 42 frost cycles affected the soil at a depth of 1 cm during a two-year period; at a depth of 10 cm only the annual frost cycle was experienced. French reflects current opinion in stating that 'one must seriously question the effectiveness of short-term freeze–thaw processes in promoting rock weathering both near the surface and at depth in all present-day periglacial environments'. The abundance of such features as block-fields in tundra and high Arctic regions may reflect (i) the very long period over which annual frost cycles have operated, and (ii) past periods of more active splitting by frost under different climatic regimes.

Quantitative assessments of frost weathering on free faces can be derived from both direct and indirect field observations. An important pioneer study was made by Rapp (1960) who measured rockfalls as they occurred from steep faces of micaschist and limestone in Kärkevagge, Lappland, during the period 1952-60. Rapp differentiated 'pebble falls' (of small fragments) from 'boulder falls' (of fragments up to several metres along the major axis). The clasts were prised away by 'frost bursting', and fell to the scree slopes beneath the rock-walls mainly during spring, as temperatures rose above $0\,^{\circ}$C and ice wedges holding the loosened fragments in position were melted. Rapp took annual 'inventories' of (i) new debris collected on fresh snow, (ii) new debris caught by vegetation on slopes, and (iii) new debris caught by sack carpets and wire netting traps at selected sites. He calculated that the average annual falls of fragments amounted to $50\,\mathrm{m}^3$ ($5\,\mathrm{m}^3$ of pebble falls; $45\,\mathrm{m}^3$ of boulder

Oversteepened valley walls resulting from Pleistocene glaciation: Swiss Alps.

falls), indicating an average annual recession of rock-walls of only 0.06 mm.

An indirect approach has yielded results of a different order of magnitude in the Swiss Alps. On the northern margins of the Glacier de Tsidjiore Nouve a large lateral moraine, comprising angular debris weathered largely from rock faces above the glacier, has accummulated during the last 5,000 years. The volume of this moraine is 9,060,000 m^3; thus there has been an average annual debris increment of 1,800 m^3. The rock faces occupy 1.55 km^2, so that the average rate of recession can be calculated as 1.16 mm per year. A significant proportion of this retreat is due to frost action; in an Alpine environment temperature fluctuations either side of 0 $^\circ$C are frequent, and meltwater from snow and ice readily penetrates joints, where it freezes to cause frost splitting. However, other processes undoubtedly contribute to rock-wall recession. Intense erosion by the Quaternary glaciers created many spectacular troughs in the Alps, with oversteepened and potentially unstable walls. With the post-glacial shrinkage of glaciers these faces were not only left unsupported but were subjected to pressure-release mechanisms. Where the resultant joints dipped down towards the valley floors sliding planes became available. These were rapidly exploited by frost action and chemical weathering, and subjected to hydrostatic pressure exerted by percolating water. In many places the shear strength of the rock was reduced to the point where stresses due to gravity could not be resisted, and large-scale rockslides and collapses occurred.

Thus in areas such as the Swiss Alps rates of slope recession due to frost weathering and allied mechanisms have been, and perhaps still are, at a maximum. In other periglacial environments where rock exposures are limited, relief is gentle and the climate relatively arid, slope retreat by frost action is minimal.

(c) Salt weathering This involves chemical processes, but its role in the disaggregation of rocks is primarily a physical one. In its commonest form salt weathering is due to crystallisation of supersaturated solutions of salts occupying fissures and pore spaces within the rock. As the crystals grow, expansive stresses are applied to joint boundaries and constituent grains, and

Small-scale exfoliation resulting from hydration: near Voi, Kenya.

surface scaling or granular disintegration can result. This type of weathering may act uniformly over the rock surface or be concentrated at particular sites (as in the formation of 'weathering pits' and 'cavernous weathering'). Salt weathering is mainly a hot-desert process, since the low rainfall and high temperatures cause salt crystals to form, with optimum effects, just beneath the surface. In the more humid tropics there is much greater *leaching* of salts, and crystallisation is inherently less likely. Nevertheless, the process may contribute to the formation of 'tafoni' (smoothly rounded caverns, with diameters of several metres, developed in shaded positions at the base of inselbergs, especially where major horizontal joints or lines of mineralogical weakness occur).

Other forms of salt weathering reported by Cooke and Warren (1973) are (i) expansion of salts within confined spaces by *heating* (which may be effective in deserts where high daytime temperatures affect salt crystals precipitated in crevices close to the rock surface), and (ii) stresses imposed by the *hydration* of salts (for example, $CaSO_4$ when hydrated expands by 0.5%). The latter process, another example of 'physico-chemical' weathering, aids scaling, exfoliation and the development of weathering pits and tafoni. In recent years salt weathering has been shown to have an important effect on building materials in desert countries.

(d) Insolation weathering It is commonly assumed that rocks are liable to fracture when subjected to large diurnal changes of temperature. Hot deserts, where daytime temperatures rise to above 40 °C and night-time temperatures can drop to 0 °C, seem to offer favourable conditions for insolation weathering. Indeed the actual rock surfaces may experience temperature fluctuations even greater than this, for when exposed directly to insolation they may heat up to 65 °C or more. The rock types most likely to be fractured by insolation weathering would seem to be (i) dark-coloured, fine-grained rocks (such as basalt), in which the low albedo ensures maximum absorption of solar energy, and (ii) heterogeneous rocks which comprise minerals with differing co-efficients of expansion.

The widespread existence of coarse and angular debris, evidently the result of physical splitting, spalling and flaking, points to the dominance of insolation weathering in hot deserts. (As shown above, the production of such detritus by frost action is probably very restricted.) However, it must be emphasised that surface changes of temperature due to insolation and radiation do not penetrate far into rocks, which are bad conductors of heat. A very thin layer (certainly not more than a few centimetres) will be stressed, and at best only small spalls or tiny exfoliation cracks can be produced. There is no possibility that large-scale exfoliation, involving sheets of rock several metres in thickness, can be detached by temperature changes; nor can large joint-bounded blocks be separated, as in block disintegration.

In fact, there is now doubt as to whether insolation weathering is significant at any scale whatsoever. Certainly laboratory experiments have failed to provide convincing evidence of the process. Griggs (1936) subjected a rock specimen to temperature changes of 110 °C for the equivalent of 244 years of diurnal heating and cooling, without any detectable disaggregation. When the specimen was cooled by water (instead of by a stream of cold dry air) surface cracking was observed after the equivalent of only $2\frac{1}{2}$ years of 'weathering'. This has been taken to indicate the possibility of chemical weathering being more potent than insolation cracking. There are, of course, problems with such experimentation. Ollier (1969) points out (i) that a laboratory specimen when heated can expand in all directions, whereas in nature it will be confined by adjacent rock so that stress can be released only in an upward direction, and (ii) that a rock which is heated and cooled for the laboratory equivalent of 244 years does not experience the same fatigue as a rock heated and cooled for an actual 244 years!

One suggestion is that the thermal expansion and contraction of rocks may cause little actual physical breakdown, but could enhance porosity and permeability; this would facilitate the entry of rainwater and assist chemical decay. Alternatively, insolation effects may merely exaggerate the stresses that already exist in a rock, owing to the process of crystallisation or formation under great pressure. In other words fracturing by pressure release may be aided by surface temperature changes. This controversy and ambiguity is very similar to that concerning the extent to which 'frost wedging' can be considered a viable process.

Block disintegration of granite: near Ilorin, western Nigeria.

Chemical weathering processes

Chemical weathering embraces a wide variety of reactions, some simple and some highly complex, which alter the chemical composition of rock minerals. Frequently these processes operate selectively, attacking certain minerals more readily than others and leading to the disaggregation of the rock into individual crystals or clusters of crystals (as in granular disintegration). Alternatively, in well jointed and bedded rocks chemical weathering will initially focus on fissures which permit the ready ingress of water and air. This will produce a larger-scale fragmentation of the rock – indeed block disintegration is often due primarily to chemical weathering, notably in warm moist climates.

As stated already (p. 15) chemical weathering is favoured by high temperatures and abundance of moisture. However, it is important that where groundwater is involved this should continually be renewed, for the reason that chemical reactions cease when dissolved salts increase to the extent that 'equilibrium' conditions obtain. It is possible that this state is approached within permanently saturated rock; indeed there is a widespread belief that the water-table marks the transition from weathering above (in the vadose zone) to 'non-weathering' below, and that this is an explanation of the basal surface of weathering beneath some deep regoliths. However, this is an over-simplification, for minerals such as feldspars are known to undergo some alteration beneath the water-table, albeit at slow rates. Weathering is certainly more rapid where there is periodic wetting and drying (as in the vadose zone, or in the zone of water-table fluctuation); this not only ensures the arrival of 'fresh' aggressive groundwater, but allows for the steady leaching of solutes. Chemical weathering may be particularly intense at the base of steep slopes owing to (i) periodic wetting by water draining off the slopes, and (ii) periodic wetting by a fluctuating water-table that at this point most closely approaches the ground surface.

The following reactions are commonly involved in chemical weathering.

(a) Solution This is a very basic weathering process, affecting unaltered rock minerals as well as weathering products. Its effectiveness is frequently determined by the acidity or alkalinity of the groundwater. Where conditions are highly alkaline ($pH > 9$) some types of silica and alumina (Al_2O_3) are readily taken into solution. Where conditions are neutral, alumina is insoluble, though its solubility will again increase with marked acidity ($pH < 4$).

(b) Carbonation   This includes the process whereby calcium carbonate ($CaCO_3$) is changed to calcium bicarbonate ($Ca(HCO_3)_2$) by rainwater containing dissolved carbon dioxide (H_2CO_3); the bicarbonate is itself readily removed in solution. However, carbonation can take other forms (for instance, carbonation occurs in feldspar weathering, the reaction between carbonic acid and potassium hydroxide giving soluble potassium carbonate).

(c) Hydration   This results from the capacity of certain minerals to take up (adsorb) water. In the process volumetric changes take place, setting up physical stresses and causing physical disaggregation. Common types of hydration are (i) the conversion of unhydrated calcium sulphate (anhydrite) to hydrated calcium sulphate (gypsum), and (ii) the conversion of iron oxides to iron hydroxides.

(d) Hydrolysis   In contrast to hydration this involves a chemical reaction between rock minerals and water; specifically there is combination between the H and OH ions of the water and the ions of the mineral. The process is very important in initiating the decomposition of feldspar, a constituent of granite, which is broken down by water into aluminosilicic acid and potassium hydroxide. The latter is carbonated and removed in solution; the former, chemically unstable, breaks down into clay minerals and silicic acid (also removed in solution). The end-product of feldspar weathering is the formation of residual clays, notably kaolinite (though it should be noted that this can also result from metamorphism during the emplacement of the granite).

(e) Oxidation and reduction   These are the processes of combining with, or dissociating from, oxygen; oxidation itself usually involves water in which oxygen is dissolved. Iron minerals are very prone to oxidation. The 'reduced' form of iron (FeO) is oxidised in free-draining, well aerated soil and regoliths to give 'oxidised iron' (FeO_3); the latter is soluble only under conditions of extreme acidity ($pH < 3$), and is therefore readily precipitated. The process accounts for the striking red and reddish-brown colours of tropical soils and regoliths.

(f) Chelation   This highly complex process involves the formation of organic acids from decaying vegetation; these acids have a marked effect on the solubility of certain elements, notably iron. The latter can be taken up by growing plants (which are in effect using 'chelating agents' to extract nutrient from the soil), or can be leached through the soil, as in podsolisation.

The formation of regoliths by chemical weathering

Unlike physical weathering, which is impeded and eventually halted if the resultant detritus is not continually transported away to give renewal of exposure, chemical weathering can over a long period result in the accumulation of deep regoliths. These are not formed everywhere; where relief is considerable, slopes steep, transport rapid, and (for reasons of temperature and humidity) rates of chemical decay only moderate, there will be an approximate equilibrium between production of regolith and its removal. This applies, for example, to much of lowland Europe at the present day (deep regoliths found here are usually relict, dating from the warmer and moister climatic conditions prevailing in the Late-Tertiary). However, in

Core-stones from deeply weathered granite: near Kuala Lumpur, western Malaysia.

many tropical and sub-tropical regions chemical weathering has 'outpaced' transportation, and regoliths of 60 m or more are sometimes found. Ruxton and Berry (1961) state that depths of rock decay are commonly in the order of 30 m in the humid tropics, 25 m in the wetter savannas, 6 m in the drier savannas, and less than 3 m in the arid zone. Deep regoliths are best developed beneath areas of gentle relief, where removal of weathered materials by streams and wash processes is ineffective. Limitations to regolith development here are imposed by (i) the duration of the weathering phase, and (ii) the 'closing up' of joints at depths of 60–90 m. The very existence of the regolith can itself reinforce chemical weathering. It is often composed of an admixture of sands and clays, whose permeability is enhanced by solution and eluviation of fines, so that acidulated rainwater can freely penetrate to the regolith–rock interface.

The chemical rotting of granite in Hong Kong has been studied by Ruxton and Berry (1957); their conclusions are broadly applicable to the weathering of crystalline rocks in many tropical humid environments. Initially rainwater penetrates joints, micro-fissures and crystal boundaries, selectively attacking rock minerals. Biotite and plagioclase feldspar are decayed quite rapidly; when the plagioclase is partly decomposed, weathering of the orthoclase feldspar begins and the rock starts to break into a mass of tiny plate-like fragments or *gruss*. At an early stage the semi-decomposed granite will display original structures (such as quartz banding and joints), but as the orthoclase is increasingly rotted the gruss will crumble into a structureless mixture of clay, silt and sand referred to as *residual debris*. The weathering of the granite will not be uniform. Large joint-bounded blocks will be detached from bedrock and slowly weathered inwards; these will then 'float' in the regolith as rounded core-stones. As the regolith progressively thickens leaching and eluviation will become important. The Hong Kong granite contains an average 36% quartz by weight; samples of residual debris contained 56% quartz, providing a measure of the removal of weathered feldspar and biotite. One result is that the surface of the regolith becomes pitted and uneven owing to subsidence.

Ruxton and Berry suggest that a fully developed regolith will comprise four 'weathering zones' (Fig. 2.2). Zone I (the uppermost) will consist of

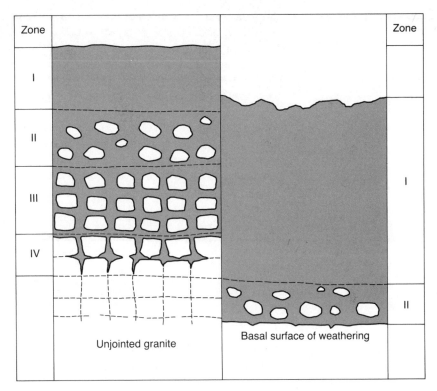

Fig. 2.2 Deep weathering profiles in granite: mature (left) and advanced (right) (based on B. P. Ruxton and L. Berry 1957 and 1961).

Zone

I

II

III

IV

Unjointed granite

Basal surface of weathering

Zone

I

II

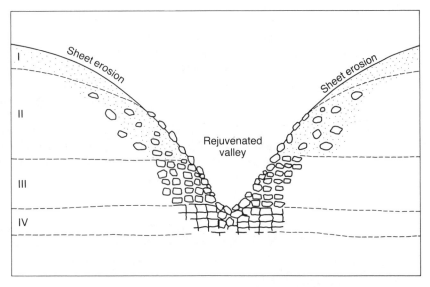

Fig. 2.3 Slope development in dissected granite weathering zones (after B. P. Ruxton and L. Berry 1957).

I

Sheet erosion

II

III

IV

Rejuvenated valley

Sheet erosion

residual debris – stable quartz sand and clay minerals such as kaolinite and sericite – containing no unweathered rock masses. It will vary in thickness from 1 to 25 m. Zone II comprises residual debris and gruss, together with rounded core-stones which occupy up to 50% of the zone (thickness up to 60 m). Zone III is made up of gruss and large numbers of rectangular core-stones, which although detached from bedrock reflect the joint structure of the granite (thickness 7–17 m). Zone IV (the lowermost) is partially weathered granite, resulting from initial penetration and opening up of joints. Ruxton and Berry argue that, with time, the upper zones will tend to increase in thickness at the expense of the lower zones, particularly where a lower limit to weathering is set by a factor such as the absence of joints.

Although deep weathering of this kind is favoured by land surface stability, many actual regoliths have experienced subsequent disturbance. In Hong Kong the weathering profile has been both fluvially dissected, as a result of Plio-Pleistocene changes of sea-level, and truncated locally by sheet erosion due to deforestation and agricultural misuse. Streams have cut deep V-shaped valleys into the regolith (Fig. 2.3); these often expose Zones III and IV, which give rise to steep boulder-strewn slopes for the reason that the weathered granite retains its coherence and resists mass slumping. Zone II (in which mass movements are more likely) is exposed on moderate-angled slopes, which have in many places been modified by sheet erosion. With the development of a 'new' pattern of relief, the weathering profile is being adjusted to the new conditions; for instance, beneath hills and interfluves the boundary between Zones I and II has become convex upwards (mirroring surface form), while the lower horizons have so far retained their near-horizontal form.

Conclusions

Weathering is, both directly and indirectly, a vital factor in slope development. Indeed it is the primary cause of slope recession, in that it alters solid and sometimes mechanically strong rock to grades of material that are amenable to transportation by mass movements and running water. The main product of weathering is a waste layer, variable in composition and thickness, that mantles most slopes; the principal exceptions are steep free faces from which weathered materials fall soon after detachment, or gentler slopes from which debris has been stripped by some form of accelerated erosion, following rejuvenation, deforestation and other kinds of interference by man.

However, it is important to emphasise that although weathering processes determine the input of rock detritus into the slope system they are in turn dependent on other processes operative within the system. Where the production of waste by weathering is rapid, and transportational processes relatively ineffective, debris will accumulate, masking the rock surface and cushioning it from atmospheric temperature changes. In these circumstances physical weathering may cease entirely. By contrast, where transport is efficient renewal of exposure of the fresh rock will favour rapid rates of weathering and slope retreat. As Rapp (1960) states in his study of rock-wall recession, the production of waste from steep faces reflects the 'local maximum rate of mechanical weathering in firm bedrock'.

3 Transport processes and the slope system

There are times when even the most academic research journals come vividly to life. One example is an account of the 4 May landslide at Saint-Jean-Vianney (Quebec, Canada) by F. Tavenas *et al*. (1971). The crucial stages in this landslide are described from the viewpoint of Mr J. Girard, who at 10.55 p.m. on that day was driving a bus around the corner of Stanley Street (Fig. 3.1). 'At this moment Mr Girard saw what appeared to be a gully in the gravel surface of the street and slowed down to drive over it. However, as the front wheels of the bus reached this gully, the soil in front of the vehicle just "disappeared" and the bus got stuck on the edge of the slide with its front wheels in the air. Mr Girard then ordered the 18 passengers to escape through the rear door . . . and reports having run on what seemed like "moving stairs" for about 150 ft (~45 m). Evidently the slide was progressing at the same speed as he was.'

Mr Girard lived to become a piece of geomorphological evidence, but 31 other people together with 40 houses, one bus and an undetermined number of cars were transported to oblivion in a mass of 7 million cubic metres of clay which flowed and scoured 3 km down valley that night and ended up at the bottom of the Saguenay River. Although traumatic for those immediately involved, this event was by no means extreme in either scale or rate of development – though Fig. 3.1 shows it to be quite impressive on both counts. Its importance in the present context lies in the way in which it draws our attention to a number of characteristics of slope transport. The processes involved vary enormously from extremely large rapid movements to extremely slow micro-scale displacement. The result is denudation in the source area, frequent erosion along the transport path, and then deposition, the degree of whose permanence varies widely. The consequent transfer of material inevit-

Fig. 3.1 Saint-Jean-Vianney landslide, 4 May 1971 (adapted from F. Tavenas *et al*.).

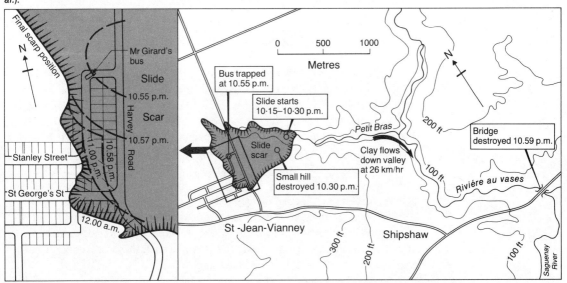

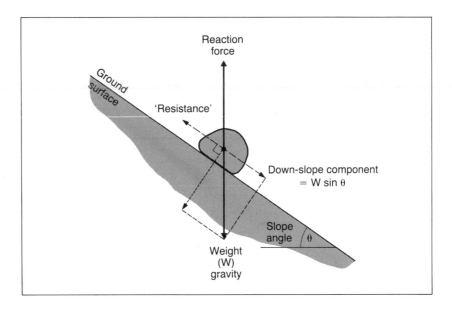

Fig. 3.2 Force of gravity acting on a slope particle.

ably leads to changes of slope morphology, and can often have direct applied implications.

Finally, Saint-Jean-Vianney demonstrates that both pure and applied geographers need to be able to understand the detailed operation of processes if they are to be capable of understanding and managing the landscape. What actually happened to the ground on the night of 4 May 1971? Why did a slope that previously appeared stable suddenly fail so dramatically? Such questions about the nature and cause of slope transport processes are of great interest and importance, but they often defy confident answers. The processes are complex, the evidence is ambiguous, and research opinions differ considerably. Our immediate task, therefore, is not to list a series of simple facts about transport processes, but rather to show what present ideas suggest might be important relationships. We can do this conveniently by considering the forces which act upon slope material and induce movement, the types of movement which result, and the rates of activity which have been found under different conditions. It will then be possible to assess the importance of transport processes both on the slope and at its foot.

The forces which produce transport on slopes

The weathering processes considered in Chapter 2 render particles of soil or rock ready for transportation. Whether or not these particles are actually moved then depends on the relative balance between the *forces* which tend to induce movement and the *resistance* (or 'reaction force') which tends to prevent it. In the simplest case we can imagine that a particle resting on a slope is subject to the forces shown in Fig. 3.2. The gravitational force acts vertically downwards and is proportional to the weight of the particle. It must be exactly balanced by an upwards reaction force, since the particle is neither rising nor falling. Clearly only a part of each of these forces acts parallel to the slope, and it is simple to demonstrate that this down-slope component of gravity equals $W \sin \theta$, where θ is the ground slope angle and W is the weight. Since the particle is still at rest, the down-slope force must be balanced by an up-slope resistance.

Several other forces are at work on the particle. As well as the direct action

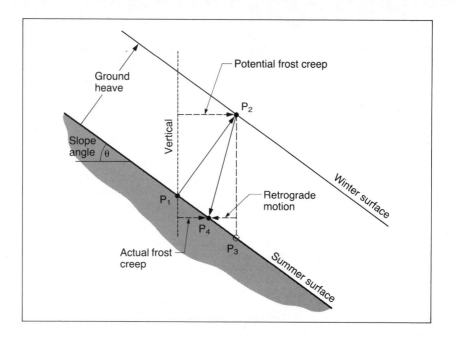

Fig. 3.3 Frost creep by expansion and contraction.

of gravity there may also be an indirect effect which operates through a transporting medium such as flowing water, raindrop impact, wind or moving ice. If we add the 'push' given by other particles moving from above, together with the impact of animal treading and vehicles, we can see that the combined forces acting on the particle may be large and that the resistance offered by the reaction force must also be large if the particle is to remain at rest.

Before considering the nature of this resistance to movement, we must note another set of processes which tend to produce down-slope motion through an alternation of expansion and contraction. An obvious example is provided by annual frost heave, a ground process related to the frost weathering that has already been discussed. Regardless of the controversy surrounding the precise mechanism of such weathering, there is general agreement that moist ground that freezes is subject to volumetric swelling, and that this expansion is released by heaving up the ground surface. The amount of heave which takes place each winter is usually 5 cm or less, though extreme values in excess of 40 cm have been recorded. The processes involved have been recognised since the 1920s, but were particularly clearly formulated by A. L. Washburn (1967) as shown in Fig. 3.3. Ground heave lifts a surface particle from P1 to P2, thus providing a 'potential frost creep' in a horizontal direction. In theory, ground subsidence during the next thaw season would be entirely gravity-controlled, so that the particle would drop vertically to P3 to complete the down-slope transport. In practice, the cohesion of the material is such that settlement is not quite vertical, and the particle thus undergoes a 'retrograde motion' to end up at P4. Thus *actual frost creep* is somewhat less than *potential frost creep*. The amount of potential frost creep is obviously proportional to the slope angle, but because of both the retrograde motion and the fact that frost creep is almost always combined with other processes, data for actual frost creep are difficult to isolate. Values of around 1–2 cm a year may be typical.

If ground expansion due to freezing can induce down-slope movement, it follows that any other process of expansion may do the same. Possible alternatives include heating and cooling, the water pressure resulting from periodic saturation of the pore spaces in a sediment, and the wetting and drying of a soil's clay content. All of these tend to be climatically controlled processes, whilst in some senses the activity of burrowing animals bringing soil to the surface might be regarded as having a similar effect for non-climatic reasons.

It is clear that a particle at rest on the slope is in fact likely to be subject to a number of forces tending to move it down slope. Whether or not actual movement takes place depends upon the magnitude of the reaction force that tends to resist movement. Since the resulting transport reflects the balance between force and resistance, we must consider what properties give material the ability to oppose movement. Two components are important, friction and cohesion. Friction occurs whenever two bodies tend to move differentially, and in the case of solid particles can be regarded as resulting from the microscopic and large-scale roughness of the surfaces which tends to lock the particles together. On a slope, friction varies with the weight of the particle and the tangent of slope angle. Cohesion gives additional 'strength' to material in the form of a variety of chemical and physical properties which bind the individual constituents together. The more cohesive the material, the greater must be the force needed to dislodge particles and move them down slope. In practice this implies that more cohesive materials need much steeper slopes to induce transport and the slope modification which is its consequence. The implications of this relationship in terms of the influence of rock type on slope are further developed in Chapter 6. Chapter 2 is also relevant in this context, since one of the main results of weathering is to change the chemical and physical cohesion of slope materials, thereby altering (and usually reducing) their resistance to transport.

The importance of cohesion as a force resisting transport is well demonstrated by the fact that the Saint-Jean-Vianney 'landslide' was actually a flow which occurred when the clay subsoil completely lost its cohesion. The ultimate cause of such events, which are by no means uncommon, remains controversial. It has traditionally been thought that the strength of such postglacial marine clays rests on their included salt crystals. When this salt is leached out by groundwater the clay particles collapse and the material *liquefies*. A more recent suggestion is that it is the lack of true clay-size (i.e. exceptionally small) particles in sediments deposited in proglacial estuarine environments that weakens the material, since many sediments rely on physical and chemical bonds between clay particles for their strength. Such discussion is far from being simply of academic interest – lives and property are at risk.

Before completing this brief introduction to the forces acting on particles, it is important to note that the account so far has been simplified by the notion that we are dealing with discrete particles sliding over plane surfaces. In reality, a debris layer is more likely to be composed of partly embedded particles as shown in Fig. 3.4 (which is drawn for a horizontal surface, though the principle can easily be extended to apply to sloping ground). In such cases a force (F) exerted on a particle of weight (W) will be resisted by the particle having to turn about a pivot. Forces acting about pivots are known as *moments* about that point. The transporting moment is thus proportional to Fd (where d is the vertical distance from pivot to particle centre), whilst the resistance (due to the weight) to be overcome is proportional to WD (where D is the horizontal distance from pivot to particle centre). The result is that the more embedded a particle becomes between its neighbours, the greater is the resistance compared with the transporting moment, and the greater will be the down-slope force needed to produce movement. The position becomes still

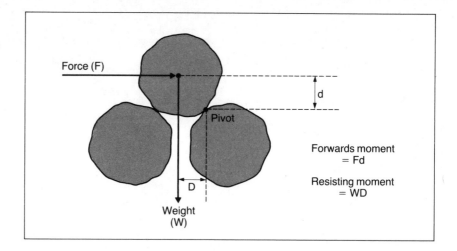

Fig. 3.4 Moments of forces acting on a particle on a rough surface.

Force (F)

d

Pivot

Forwards moment
= Fd

Resisting moment
= WD

D

Weight
(W)

more complex when the transporting force is in the form of a medium such as flowing water or wind, since the velocities achieved at the boundary layer with such particles vary greatly on a micro-scale. The resulting pattern of transport is in detail the subject of much research at the present time.

Types of slope transport process

Whilst engineers have long regarded slope transport as a problem of forces acting on materials, this viewpoint has only recently found favour amongst geomorphologists. The traditional geomorphological approach has concentrated on the resulting slope morphology and rate of change, and has used this as evidence from which to deduce ideas about the actual mechanisms involved. We shall see in Chapter 8 that these two viewpoints are complementary rather than conflicting, and that each has both merits and weaknesses. The most fundamental division of transport processes is between those which rely on the action of some external agent (of which flowing water is the most important), and those mass movement processes which involve only the surface deposits themselves.

1 Slope-wash and related processes

We can use this general heading to include all types of transport by water on the slope, except those which involve concentration of water into gullies, at

Infiltration excess flow on unvegetated steep slopes: Arizona, U.S.A.

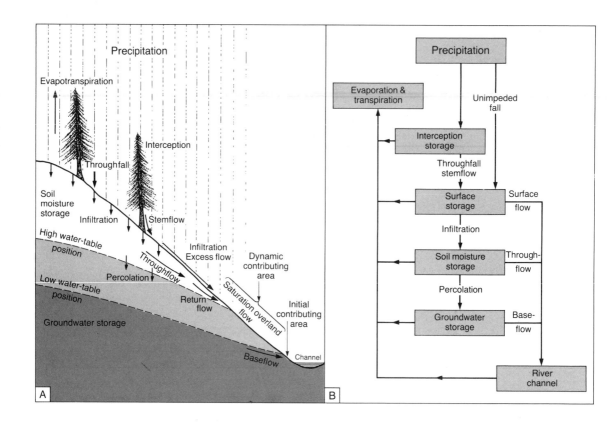

Fig. 3.5 Slope hydrology.

which stage marked incision of the slope begins and thus constitutes a channel process that is best considered separately. The amount of transport achieved by wash-related processes will depend on slope angle, the erodibility of the surface material, vegetation cover and the amount of water involved. An understanding of this aspect of slope process is therefore directly linked to a consideration of slope hydrology.

Rain falling upon a slope will either be returned to the atmosphere by evapotranspiration, or must be removed by surface flow (with general potential for transport) or sub-surface flow (significant mainly for the transport of dissolved material). Fig. 3.5A shows that this simple initial idea (WATER INPUT = WATER OUTPUT) is in fact quite complicated in detail, since water may also be *stored* in various ways and these stores 'buffer' the relationship between input and output (so that INPUT = OUTPUT ± CHANGE IN STORAGE). The geomorphologically significant pattern of sediment transport and removal depends on the relative importance of the various stores and the rates of water transfer between them in any particular area. Fig. 3.5B shows the same components in a rather more abstract form which in fact depicts the operation of the hydrological system (or 'hydrological cycle'). Thus whilst hydrologists and fluvial geomorphologists would regard this system as controlling the *input* of water and sediment to the channel network, slope geomorphologists would view it as defining the *throughput* and *output* of slope water and sediment – with important repercussions for slope form and development.

Precipitation is either intercepted by vegetation, or falls directly to the ground. The water trapped by plants may be evaporated, or may in turn pass by *stemflow* and *throughfall* to the surface. It is therefore clear that vegetation acts as a control both on the amount of water reaching the ground, and on the rate and impact with which it is received at the surface. As research effort is increasingly directed towards this relationship, it is being found that

Zones of slope-wash and
gully action on a badland
slope: Arizona, U.S.A.

the role of vegetation as a control of surface flow and sediment yield is more
complex and more important than had been suspected. Thus changes in
vegetation cover, whether natural or man-made, may be regarded as major
influences on slope process at both the meso- and micro-scale.

There may be some short-term storage of water in surface depressions but
most is quickly removed by evaporation or, more significantly in the slope
context, by infiltration and surface flow. Unfortunately, the terminology
used by different researchers for these processes has become markedly confused. In the early stages of the development of these ideas, slope geomorphologists and channel hydrologists both tended to think simply in terms of
a single type of surface flow that could be termed loosely 'surface run-off' or
'overland flow'. More recently it has been appreciated that, particularly in
humid areas, surface flow takes two forms which have differing location,
duration, intensity and transportational ability. The first relates to the rate
at which water can infiltrate into the ground, and for our purposes can be
called *infiltration excess flow* (or 'Horton overland flow' after R. E. Horton
who introduced the idea in 1945). The second relates to complete saturation
of the ground and can thus conveniently be called *saturation overland flow*.
It is important to consider these two components separately.

The rate at which water can infiltrate into the soil is controlled by the *infiltration capacity*, often expressed in millimetres per hour. Infiltration capacity
varies greatly in natural soils, commonly being limited to 100–150 mm per
hour, but in extreme cases exceeding 2,000 mm per hour. It rises as grain and
pore size increase, and also with good vegetation cover (which reduces soil
compaction by raindrops and delivers water to the ground at a more even rate)
and low slope angle (which gives water more time to sink in). It is usually at
a maximum when soil is almost dry, close to the commencement of rainfall,
and thereafter is progressively reduced, though occasionally complete soil
desiccation has the opposite effect and impedes initial infiltration. It follows
that infiltration capacity is highly variable in space and time. Since surface
flow represents that portion of the water not removed by evapotranspiration
or infiltration this, too, is subject to great variability. Factors which tend to
increase infiltration excess flow across the surface will understandably include
any property which reduces infiltration capacity, such as small grain and pore

33

size, absence of vegetation and steep slope angle. Since actual precipitation rate only rarely exceeds 100 mm per hour, it can be seen that this type of surface flow is unlikely to be important except under the most extreme storm conditions.

The other type of surface flow, saturation overland flow, occurs when soil pore spaces are completely filled with water so that infiltration is reduced almost to zero (strictly it is reduced to the small amount necessary to replenish the soil water moving away beneath the surface). This can be caused by relatively impermeable soil layers retarding downward percolation close to the surface, or may be related to a rise of the ground water-table to meet the surface. The water stored in the soil above the water-table may percolate downwards or be removed laterally by *throughflow*, another process which is increasingly being recognised as playing a vital role in slope hydrology and geomorphology, especially within humid areas. Some throughflow takes place rapidly, either along zones of concentrated percolation (known as 'percolines') or through actual soil pipes. This rapid movement is capable of transporting solid and solute load. Slower diffuse throughflow also takes place though its transportational role is largely limited to solutes. As evidence mounts for the geomorphological significance of these processes, it becomes clear that even the slight permeability contrasts of different soil horizons may influence slope transport.

Some water continues to percolate downwards to join the groundwater store, from which *baseflow* of water keeps rivers flowing in between rainfall events. Whilst the water-table (which represents the top of the groundwater storage) usually intersects the surface close to the river channel, it is subject to a significant rise after rainfall so as to meet the surface part of the way up the valley slope. All areas down slope of this point of intersection will experience saturation overland flow. A rise of water-table thus greatly increases the total amount of surface flow. The area producing saturation overland flow increases progressively through a major rainfall event. This *dynamic contributing area* concept of surface flow production has been used by hydrologists since the 1960s, but is now seen as being of equal geomorphological interest in helping to explain the changing pattern of sediment removal. The suggestion that solute load has greater denudational significance than was traditionally recognised is also important here, for the fluctuating water-table may enhance chemical weathering and encourage the uptake of solutes.

Although slope hydrology represents a major focus for future research, it has already become clear that Horton's traditional view that 'overland flow' (which he regarded largely as a product of precipitation exceeding infiltration) regularly occurs on slopes except for a narrow belt along the crest (an idea discussed on pp. 32–33) is an over-simplification. On those parts of the slope not experiencing surface flow within the dynamic contributing area (an important component of which may comprise a *return flow* fed by throughflow to the surface near the slope-foot), it may generally be the case that greater attention should be paid to the direct action of raindrops in breaking down soil aggregates and moving particles down slope. Recent work in this field using simulated rainfall has emphasised the significance of soil erodibility, and has tended to play down the importance of surface flow except on steep bare slopes. As well as having important academic implications, such work impinges directly on studies of 'accelerated erosion' or 'soil erosion' which have great practical importance.

Fig. 3.6 Carson and Kirkby's classification of mass movement processes.

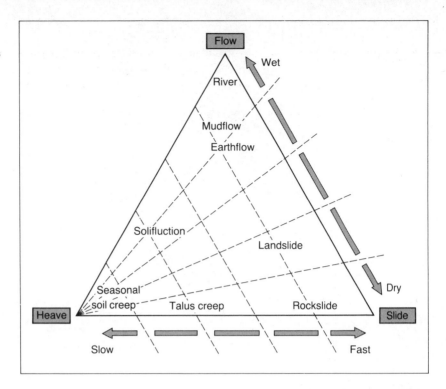

Fig. 3.7 Types of mass movement: flow (A) and slide (B).

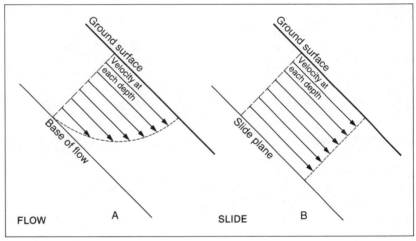

2 *Mass movement*

Mass movement is a general term for all those processes which induce transport of slope material in response to the forces discussed earlier rather than as a result of entrainment by water or wind. Mass movements show great variety of scale, rate, material and resulting landforms. Many different classifications have been proposed using these criteria, and for our purposes it is necessary to adopt a simplified structure. A more detailed treatment is provided by Finlayson and Statham (1980), and by Carson and Kirkby (1972) who developed the classification shown in Fig. 3.6. They recognise three main types of movement, *heave* (Fig. 3.3), *flow* and *slide* (Figs 3.7A and 3.7B), and then use these as a basic for classifying the main types of slope processes. It will be seen that this classification excludes rockfall which is experienced

Fig. 3.8 Rockfall and talus
development.

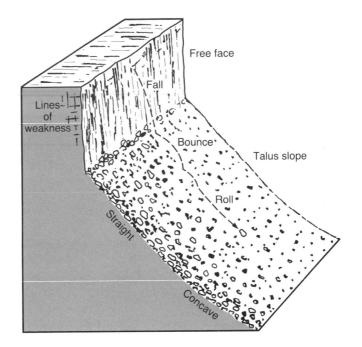

Free face

Fall

Lines-
of
weakness

Bounce

Talus slope

Roll

Straight

Concave

Rockfall.

(Above right)
Rectilinear talus slopes:
Rocky Mountains, Colorado.

Concave base of avalanche
talus cone: Swiss Alps.

Fig. 3.9 Rockslide.

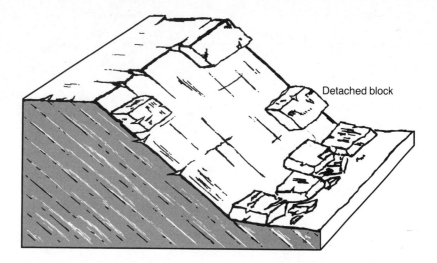

Detached block

by individual particles rather than by surface material moving as a mass, but for convenience we can add this process to our list. The main types of mass movement are discussed briefly below, divided into four categories.

(a) Rockfall and toppling   These take place on the steepest bare rock slopes (angles greater than 40°) where detached fragments will fall and bounce rather than roll or slide. Most falls involve individual fragments which may disintegrate on impact, but occasional major slope collapses take place. Steep mountain slopes ('free faces') and coastal cliffs are the most common sites for rockfalls (Fig. 3.8). Many rocks would have strength to sustain cliffs much higher than those which occur naturally were it not for the presence of joints, faults and fissures which offer lines of weakness along which detachment of blocks is facilitated. A number of processes are thought to be responsible for actually triggering a particular fall, including thermal or freezing expansion, water pressure in pores or joints, pressure-release jointing and chemical activity. Since several of these processes are climate-related there is often a seasonal pattern of rockfalls, with a maximum in spring and autumn. Some major falls may be triggered by an external event such as an earthquake or severe coastal storm.

Falls are significant both in producing recession of steep rock walls and in providing the debris which feeds the screes and talus slopes often found at the foot of a free face. Although talus slopes have traditionally been regarded as straight slopes at the *angle of rest* of the debris (i.e. the angle beyond which the debris would become unstable and start rapid movement), it is now realised that most talus has a concave section at the base, and that the upper straight part is slightly gentler than might be expected. This results from the fact that rocks falling down the free face attain a high velocity and are only brought to rest when the slope across which they bounce and then roll or slide is gentler than the true frictional angle of repose. The higher the free face, the gentler will be the talus needed to bring the falling rocks to a halt.

(b) Landslides and rockslides   These affect masses of material which generally retain their coherence whilst moving across a clearly defined slide plane. As shown in Fig. 3.7B, velocity is essentially uniform throughout the sliding mass in simple cases. *Rockslides* (Fig. 3.9) affect individual masses of resistant rock, or may be very large-scale movements influencing large parts of a slope. The influence of bedding and jointing as controls of block detachment and in

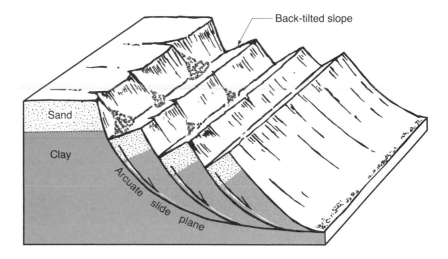

Fig. 3.10 Rotational slips.

Back-tilted slope

Sand

Clay

Arcuate slide plane

Fig. 3.11 Slump.

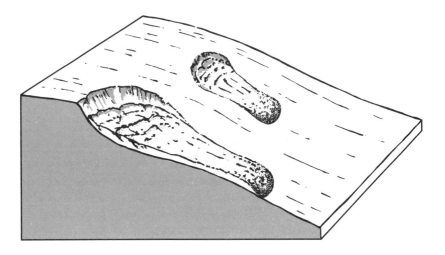

providing slide planes is paramount. It follows that structural control of the resulting slope form is strong, a point stressed in Chapter 6. *Landslides* comprise a variety of processes affecting less strong rocks, but are characterised by most of the movement taking place across a defined plane. Very shallow slides may take place after heavy rain, particularly on clay slopes, and involve mainly the weathered surface material. Clay soils subjected to movement become very weak, and may slide again if slope angle is greater than about 10°.

Deep landslides usually take place across arcuate slide planes. Although many varieties are found, two common types are *rotational slips* and *slumps*. Classic rotational slips (Fig. 3.10) are often associated with permeable cap-rocks (e.g. sandstone) overlying an impermeable substratum (e.g. clay). They characterise oversteepened slopes such as marine cliffs or actively retreating escarpments. Coherent blocks of material slip down across one or more converging slide planes so that tilted back-slopes are found at the surface and may trap sediment or standing water. Slumps (Fig. 3.11) are similar in some respects, but the coherence of the mass is lost; consequently, although there is a slide plane, movement is also taking place as a flow especially near the toe. This combination of processes produces an arcuate scar at the head where material has been evacuated, a linear tongue of mobile material, and a bulging toe dominated by flowage.

Landslides are very sensitive to water content, which reduces the strength

Rotational slump with back-tilted surface in gravel cliff: Southern England.

Unconsolidated clay slump across well marked slide plane: Southern England.

of the material by increasing water pressure in pores and joints. This has the effect of 'pushing' particles apart, thereby weakening the links between them. At the same time the water content adds weight to the material so that down-slope force is increased whilst resistance is decreased. As a consequence,

Landscape dominated by surface striping associated with solifluction: western Canadian Arctic.

landsliding reflects weather conditions, being maximised after heavy rain or snow-melt, particularly if previous desiccation has cracked the surface so as to facilitate infiltration. Climatic change may initiate a period of landsliding if wetter conditions are introduced.

The boundaries between mass movement types are not clearly defined, so that the distinction between rockfall and rockslide may lie simply in an arbitrary slope angle. Similarly there is only a very indistinct division between a wet slump and a dry flow or zone of creep.

(c) Creep and solifluction   These, again, bring together a variety of processes under a simple heading. Most creep results from the expansion and contraction processes discussed earlier, with the gravity force ensuring that the dominant movement is down-slope. In addition, clay soils may creep continuously because moist clay deforms slowly under gravitational stress. The pattern of movement in most other types of creep is discontinuous, but its overall effect is much closer to a flow (Fig. 3.7A) than to a slide (Fig. 3.7B). The depth below which the movement is reduced to zero varies greatly depending on material, slope and environment, and may range from little more than 20 cm to depths in excess of 8 metres.

'Solifluction' is an ambiguous term that has been loosely applied to surficial mass movement, particularly in periglacial areas where soil moisture content in the thaw season is very high because percolation is impeded by impermeable permafrost. Solifluction only rarely relies to any significant extent on sliding across the permafrost surface, but even so comprises a combination of two quite separate processes. Frost creep is strictly the expansion/contraction process that we have seen operates by way of frost heave (Fig. 3.3), whilst solifluction flow (or *gelifluction*) results from saturation or supersaturation of the surface material by meltwater from snow and ground ice. There is much discussion as to the relative importance of these components, and it seems likely that their ranking will depend on the grain size, water content and climate found on each particular slope.

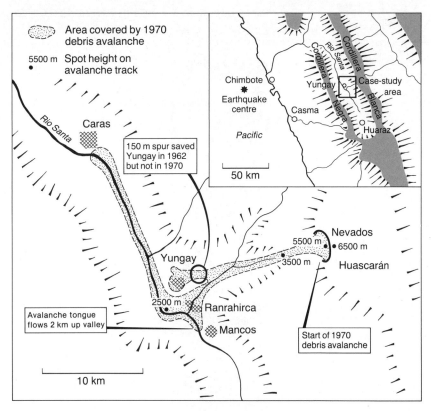

Fig. 3.12 Sketch map of 1972 debris avalanche at Yungay, Peru.

Area covered by 1970 debris avalanche

5500 m Spot height on avalanche track

Chimbote

Earthquake centre

Casma

Pacific

Yungay

Case-study area

Huaraz

50 km

Rio Santa

Caras

150 m spur saved Yungay in 1962 but not in 1970

Yungay

Nevados
5500 m • 6500 m
3500 m
Huascarán

2500 m

Ranrahirca

Avalanche tongue flows 2 km up valley

Mancos

Start of 1970 debris avalanche

10 km

(d) **Earthflow and mudflow** These may occur simply at the saturated toe of a landslide, or may form a distinctive transport type in their own right. Small flows may develop locally on saturated incoherent slope material, perhaps even taking place beneath the turf cover. Other flows may be large and rapid, increasing in speed and decreasing in necessary slope angle as water content rises. In theory, mudflows give way to sediment-laden streams with no distinct boundary, thus further blurring the distinction between slope and fluvial processes.

The Saint-Jean-Vianney 'landslide' was in fact dominated by flow of lique-fied clay, hence explaining the fact that a wall of clay 18 m high was able to move down valley at a speed of about 26 km per hour. However, as is often the case, the process was complex in that it was initiated by slumping of solid blocks of clay so that the retreating head of the feature was in the form of a steep scarp about 22 m high, on the lip of which Mr Girard's bus became suspended.

A particularly devastating form of mass movement possessing attributes of both flow and slide is the *cataclysmic rockslide* or *debris avalanche* that occurs when a very large amount of rock falls freely before impacting with the ground and pulverising. The energy released by fall and pulverisation is able to accelerate the mass to exceptionally high velocities across gentle slopes or even uphill. Such an event was triggered on the northern flank of the Rio Santa valley in the Andes of Peru (Fig. 3.12) on 31 May 1970. An earthquake dislodged an 800 m mass of ice and rock from the mountain summit of Huascarán. This fell 1,000 m before shattering on the valley floor below, releasing sufficient energy to send an enormous mass of rubble 16 km to the Rio Santa valley in 1 minute 57 seconds – an incredible 480 km per hour. In the process it crossed a spur 150 m high and devastated the town of Yungay, killing

41

Fig. 3.13 General ranges of transport velocity.

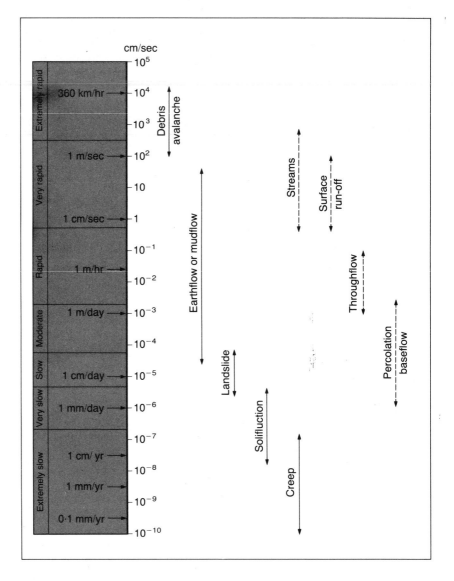

10,000 of its inhabitants. For part of its remarkable journey it apparently rose on to a cushion of air, for delicate plants and landforms in its path remained undamaged. It is clear that there is still much to be learned about slope processes, but the example is a fitting point at which to turn to a brief consideration of rates of activity.

Rate and magnitude of slope processes

The Huascarán debris avalanche demonstrates the several quite distinct attributes which combine to define the magnitude of a process - velocity (480 km per hour), volume of material (40 million cubic metres), extent of movement (some 20 km, but mainly confined to the valley bottom), depth of moving layer (10 cm to 10 m), frequency of movement (sporadic and rare, being triggered by a 7.7 Richter scale earthquake). We can use these criteria to assess the geomorphological importance of other slope processes.

Velocity

A general indication of characteristic velocities is provided by Fig. 3.13, which indicates the substantial range that exists both within and between process types. Many factors influence transport velocity, including all those properties which affect the force applied to the material or the resistance to movement that it offers. We have seen already that there are important local variations of velocity with depth (especially in flows, Fig. 3.7A) and with time (as with infiltration reduction through a storm), but perhaps most important are the influences of slope angle and of climate. Thus surface soil creep in humid temperate areas may be typically 1–2 mm per year, whilst values three times greater are common in tropical humid areas.

Volume of material

Volume is really only a meaningful measure when applied to processes which can be clearly demarcated in space and in time. Thus, though it is possible to contrast large volumes such as the 40 million cubic metres of the Huascarán debris avalanche or 7 million cubic metres of the Saint-Jean-Vianney clay flow with more common values such as 5–50 cubic metres for rockfalls, 10–100 cubic metres for debris transport by moderate snow avalanches and 50–200 cubic metres for small landslides, such data contrasts tend to draw our attention to rare extreme events, and may therefore be misleading. The geomorphological significance of a process combines amount of material and velocity of movement with the equally important consideration of the extent (spatial and temporal) of the process.

Extent and frequency of process

The amount of slope denudation performed by a process depends upon its spatial extent, its duration and its frequency of occurrence. Some types of creep are almost continuous, and may influence most of a land surface. By contrast a rock slide may last only seconds, influence only a few metres of the surface, and occur only rarely. Attempts to combine all aspects of process magnitude are uncommon, but an instructive example is the meticulous work of the Swedish geomorphologist Anders Rapp (1960) on the Kärkevagge valley in Lappland, summarised below:

Process	Annual volume (cubic metres)	Annual average movement (metres)	Annual index of denudation (see text below)
Rockfalls	50	225	19,565
Avalanches	88	150	21,850
Slides	580	0.5 to 600	76,300
Talus creep	300,000	0.01	2,700
Solifluction	550,000	0.02	5,300
Water (solutes)	150	700	136,500

In terms of simple volume, the widespread processes of talus creep and solifluction appear overwhelmingly dominant, but if the vertical distance moved by the material is taken into account to provide a general index of annual denudation (calculated by multiplying tons of material (as in the above example) by vertical distance of transport in metres), then removal of dissolved material in running water is seen to be the most significant element in this arctic mountain area. This rather surprising result has been confirmed from a number of different environments. It seems that whilst abrupt changes and clearly defined slope features may relate mainly to mass movements, if we consider overall denudation of the landscape then hydrological processes must be given high priority.

Depth of movement

Again, great variety is characteristic. Flow-related processes usually reduce quite rapidly with depth except where a plant root zone produces an added reduction higher up the profile. In extreme cases creep may extend to depths of 8 m, but solifluction is usually restricted to the topmost 40–60 cm. Earthflows and mudflows are 0.5–10 m deep, whilst deep-seated landslides may extend to several tens of metres. In a sense, depth of movement can be subsumed into volume calculations when an attempt is made to assess the overall significance of a process.

Conclusion

Although we have considered the topic relatively briefly, it is clear that slope processes are complex and often poorly understood. The engineering approach to their study tends towards over-simplification of their environmental context, whilst geomorphologists have traditionally been guilty of an over-descriptive viewpoint dominated by individual case studies. Nevertheless, since it is through the action of these processes that slopes are created and modified, we will return to them later to help explain variations of slope with climate, lithology and time. But first we must consider the problems of depicting and analysing the form and angle of the slope. Such description should not be regarded as an end in itself, but no science can develop without a firm descriptive basis.

4 Slope form and angle

At first sight the slopes of an area of even moderate relief may give an impression of rather bewildering complexity, and the primary task of slope survey is to record, depict and analyse representative information about the resulting pattern. However, whilst it is easy to make an intuitive comparison between the slopes of areas of low, moderate and high relief, the detailed description and explanation of these differences is more difficult. To ensure success, thought must be given to three problems – aim, method and technique.

An area of low relief: prairies near Drumheller, Alberta, Canada.

An area of moderate relief: near Magadi, southern Kenya.

An area of high relief: east of Arolla, Valais, Switzerland.

Survey aim – a purpose for the investigation

Why bother to survey slope form? Such surveys take some skill and much effort, and clearly need careful justification. It is relatively easy to argue that a debris avalanche is worth studying, since such investigation might save life and property, but can we really claim that there is any merit in knowing the difference between convex and concave, or any value in the distinction between $22°$ and $35°$? Surprisingly, we can find four purposes which do justify the effort.

(i) It is notoriously difficult to assess slope angle and form by eye. Try estimating the angle of the cliff and debris slope in the photograph (p. 55), then assess the maximum angle present in the area shown by the photograph (p. 56), and suggest what proportion of the slope profile is straight rather than curved. The first purpose of slope survey is to provide an objective description of such properties, which are very difficult to describe subjectively. If such description is comprehensive and accurate, it can then be used as a basis for the tasks which follow.

(ii) Slopes vary greatly from place to place in response to many factors, and a major purpose of slope geomorphology is to understand what these links are. Carefully designed slope survey can be of enormous value in this context. For example, how could we set about defining the difference between the slopes that develop on areas of sandstone and limestone? Two requirements must be met by our study if it is to be scientifically acceptable. First, all variables other than geology must be held constant (i.e. the chosen case-study areas should be identical in every respect except that one is sand-stone whilst the other is limestone). This is strictly unattainable in practice, but we can sometimes get close to achieving it. Secondly, our assessment of the slopes in each geological type must be 'replicated'. It is tempting to make a single survey on each rock type, and assume that the difference is due to geological control, but it could equally well result from another factor that we had not considered or could even be a chance product of the particular slopes we had chosen to survey. By replicating (or repeating) the surveys on each rock type and demonstrating that the sandstone surveys were similar to each other as a group, but distinct from the group of limestone surveys, we go a long way towards meeting this difficulty.

A laboratory physicist or chemist might still be tempted to reject much slope study as being an intuitive art rather than a rigorous science. However, although it is never possible in field study to match the perfect control, standardisation and replication of a laboratory experiment, it is possible with care to design a survey which offers acceptable reliability. In this way, slope form survey offers a powerful means of assessing the links between a slope and the factors which influence it.

(iii) As well as responding to present-day factors, slopes may also be considered to be a product of a sequence of evolution, though the extent to which this history of development is represented in the present form varies greatly from case to case. We shall find in Chapter 5 that the challenge of unravelling the history of a slope has long fascinated geomorphologists, but that hard evidence has often taken second place to pure speculation. If theories of slope evolution are to be refined and tested they will have to be related to the objective data provided by slope survey.

(iv) If slope form information can be used to analyse the present factors and processes at work, and to define the sequence of development in progress, it follows that it might also form a basis for predicting future changes. The ability to assess the present capability of a slope and its future behaviour in response to specified land uses offers one of the main practical applications of slope study that will be discussed in Chapter 8.

Survey method – designing the right approach

We have already mentioned some of the requirements of scientific method that a slope study must meet. It is also necessary to decide whether the study is to be focused on a single variable (slope angle is the most common) or is to be multivariate (e.g. angle, form, orientation). Finally, we must choose between a field study (affording maximum information and accuracy, but expensive and time-consuming) or a laboratory study (affording lower level of information and accuracy but rapid, wide coverage, and relatively cheap). In practice it may be possible to combine the two by undertaking a regional laboratory study using maps or air photographs, and then confirming the trends or adding to the information through selected field case studies. The chosen methodology is likely to lead to one of three kinds of data – slope map, slope profile or slope statistics. These three topics will be developed shortly.

Survey technique – putting the method into operation

Many different survey techniques are available for field or laboratory use, giving varying degrees of accuracy. In general it is necessary to compromise between the high precision and high information content that might seem ideal, and the low available finance and short time that often make this ideal unattainable. Luckily, provided that the method of approach has been carefully designed, quite simple techniques can yield useful information. Some

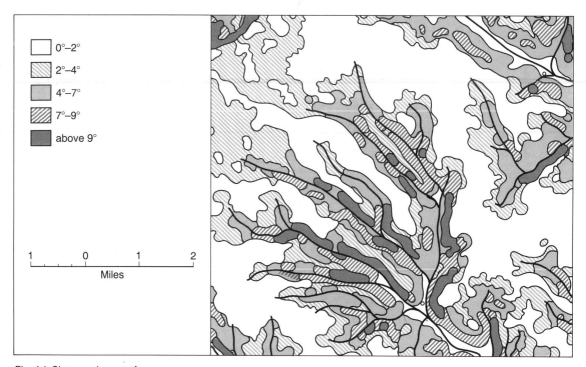

Fig. 4.1 Slope-angle map of the area near Chesham (after C. D. Ollier and A. J. Thomasson 1957).

□	0°–2°
▨	2°–4°
▨	4°–7°
▨	7°–9°
▨	above 9°

```
1      0      1      2
├──────┼──────┼──────┤
        Miles
```

suggestions on appropriate technique are made in the context of the main types of slope data discussed below.

Slope maps

Slope is usually mapped in one of three ways – slope angle, slope form (in profile and plan), and slope 'morphology' in the widest sense. *Slope-angle maps* such as that in Fig. 4.1 are less common than might be thought, given that slope is such a basic property of landscape. Small areas may be mapped in the field, but regional surveys are usually based on pre-existing contour maps on which contour spacing can be used to assess inclination. Clearly, such maps are highly simplified versions of the real world, but they do give an immediate visual impression of patterns of surface steepness, and can yield quantitative data if the areas within each slope class are measured and summed. Several techniques and innumerable angle classifications have been suggested over the years, but Demek (1972) presented the agreed version of the International Geographical Union's Commission on Geomorphological Survey and Mapping. To draw a boundary to separate the areas falling into two adjacent slope-angle classes, the contour spacing appropriate to the chosen slope angle is calculated. Dividers are set to this distance, and all places on the map where the relevant contour spacing occurs are marked and joined by an isoline which becomes the slope class boundary. The standard class intervals and terminology selected were:

0°–0° 30′	Plain
0° 30′–2°	Slightly sloping
2°–5°	Gently inclined
5°–15°	Strongly inclined (sometimes divided 5°–10°, 10°–15°)
15°–25°	Steep $\Big\}$ (sometimes combined)
25°–35°	Very steep
35°–55°	Precipitous
55°	Vertical

48

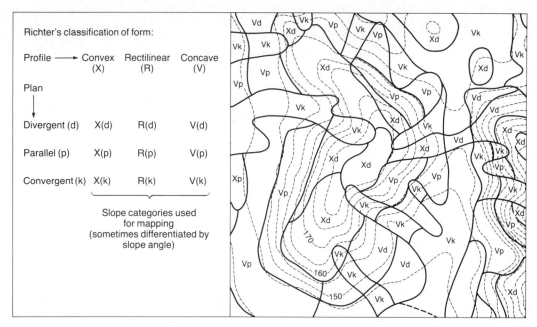

Fig. 4.2 Slope plan-form map
(after J. Demek 1972).

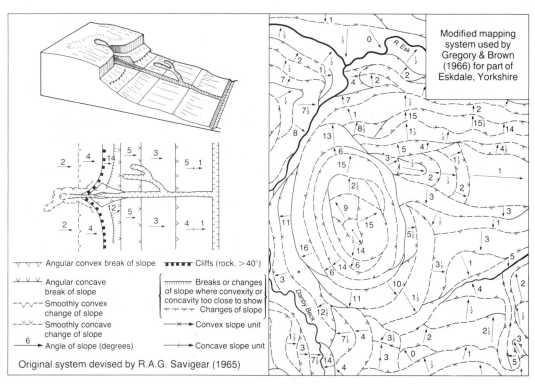

Fig. 4.3 Morphological
mapping of slopes.

The same volume demonstrates a mapping technique for *slope form* which includes both profile form (convex, concave, rectilinear) and plan form (curvature indicated by whether lines running directly down the steepest slope would be divergent as on a spur, convergent as in a valley head, or parallel). Fig. 4.2 shows how the resulting nine types of slope might be mapped. Alternatively, plan form can be specified by the radius of contour curvature.

Perhaps most common is the more generalised approach adopted by *morphological mapping* (Fig. 4.3), by which areas are divided into more or less distinct zones each combining a characteristic range of slope angle and type of form. In this context most of the information about form is given by the boundaries between classes. With this rather formal descriptive basis, symbols for other slope, channel and material characteristics can be added to the map to build up a comprehensive landscape description with both academic and practical value. A further extension is to add information about the supposed origin and age of the features depicted, thereby changing from a morphological to a *geomorphological map*. Such maps are the most informative sources, but are considerably more subjective than simple slope maps and are therefore often considered less appropriate as data for analysis or application.

Slope profiles

Whilst simple illustrative cross-sections can be constructed from contour maps to show the main features of large slopes, profiles intended for analysis as an approach to slope study have to be surveyed in the field. Three tasks are involved: selecting a profile line to be surveyed, subdividing the profile into a series of measured lengths, and surveying the distance and angle of each measured length. With this information, an accurate profile can be plotted and analysed.

Selecting the profile line   This is less straightforward than might be thought. Choosing a 'representative' profile by eye is unacceptable as a basis for scientific study, since the selection may well reflect some subconscious preconception about slope characteristics to be included. As far as is possible, a random choice should be made, perhaps based on prior study of a map. Unless there are special circumstances, valley heads and spur ends should be avoided, since these are the zones of convergent and divergent lines of debris movement down the steepest slopes mentioned in our consideration of slope-

Fig. 4.4 Classification of slope for survey purposes, with suggested locations for profiles.

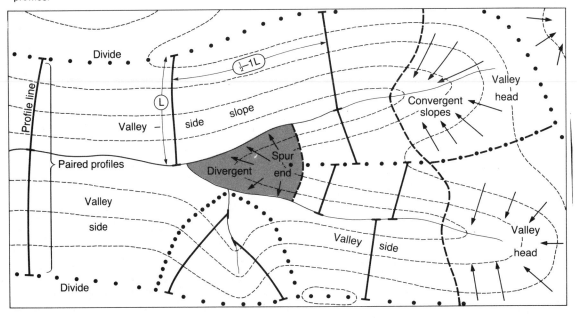

Fig. 4.5 Measured length for
slope survey.

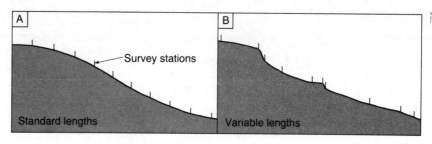

Fig. 4.6 Slope survey
measurements.

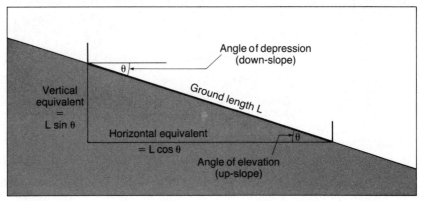

form mapping above. Since the slope profile is a product of debris transport, erosion and deposition, the most easily interpretable profile lines are those which run directly down the steepest slopes in areas where the slope is straight in plan (Fig. 4.4). The profile line is at best likely to be straight only in its central portion, and will curve to join the crest and valley bottom. Keeping the profile at right angles to the contours is easy on a map, but much more difficult in the field. It has been found that surveying downwards from the slope crest is the most accurate method. In order to keep each profile independent of its neighbours, profile lines should be spaced at a distance equal to or half the profile length.

Subdividing the profile   Subdivision into measured lengths is approached in one of two ways. Unless there are good reasons for doing otherwise, the surveyor uses a standard length (Fig. 4.5A) so that each surveyed distance is the same. The recommended length is 5 m, though for particularly short or long slopes alternative values of 2 m, 10 m or 20 m might be selected. There are occasions (Fig. 4.5B) where a standard-length method is replaced by use of variable lengths selected subjectively so as to avoid missing important slope features. This is an effective method for surveying illustrative profiles, but introduces technical and subjectivity problems when the aim is to use the profiles for statistical analysis.

Surveying angle and distance of each measured length   This task must be done next. Fig. 4.6 shows that angles can be measured up slope (elevation) or down slope (depression), and that the ground distance actually measured can be simply used to yield vertical and horizontal equivalent. It is rarely necessary to measure distances more accurately than to the nearest 0.1 m, and rarely possible to measure angles to better than $\frac{1}{2}°$ except by the very time-consuming use of sophisticated equipment. Most slope surveys use an Abney level or clinometer for angle measurement, or (for medium or short slopes) take both angle and distance from a slope pantometer. Fig. 4.7A demonstrates

51

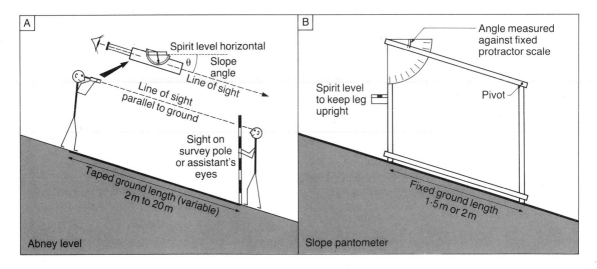

Fig. 4.7 Techniques for measuring slope angles.

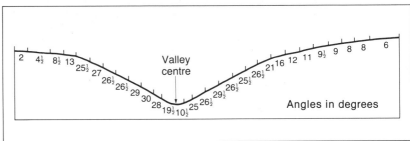

Fig. 4.8 Plotted slope profiles.

the principle of Abney or clinometer survey, and shows that whilst it is possible for one person to work with a graduated ranging rod there are considerable time advantages in using a team of two people. Pantometer survey (Fig. 4.7B) is very quick and surprisingly accurate, though it has the disadvantage of a very short measured length (1.5 m or 2 m) and has drawbacks on rough ground. Other methods are available, and full details are given by Young (1974). Whilst geomorphologists usually measure angles in degrees, engineers and geologists often use percentage slope. A conversion table is shown below:

Degrees	Percentage	Degrees	Percentage
0°	0%	10°	17.6%
1°	1.8%	20°	34.4%
2°	3.5%	30°	57.7%
3°	5.2%	40°	83.9%
4°	7.0%	45°	100%
5°	8.8%	50°	119.2%
6°	10.5%	60°	173.2%
7°	12.3%	70°	274.8%
8°	14.1%	80°	567.1%
9°	15.8%	90°	∞

Profile plotting and analysis   This is based upon the survey observations. A plotted profile (Fig. 4.8) gives an immediate visual image of the slope concerned, but analysis must be based upon something more rigorous than simple visual comparison. Further consideration of the slope-angle

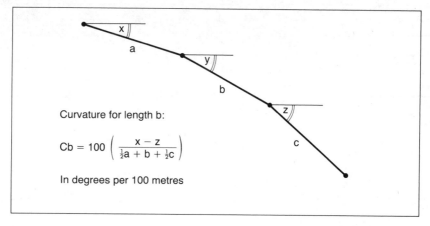

Fig. 4.9 Calculation of profile curvature.

Curvature for length b:

$$Cb = 100 \left(\frac{x - z}{\frac{1}{2}a + b + \frac{1}{2}c} \right)$$

In degrees per 100 metres

information is given in the context of slope statistics in the next section, but analysis of profile form can conveniently be dealt with here since the treatment is often more qualitative and subjective.

The first task is to classify the profile into rectilinear units (which are called *segments*) and curved units (called *elements*, and subdivided into *convex* and *concave* types). This can be achieved simply by using a ruler to designate all those segments which are approximately straight, thus by elimination leading to an identification of the elements. Such an approach is difficult to standardise, particularly if different studies are to be compared. To make the classification more objective it is necessary to adopt a statistical examination of the amount of angular variation with a proposed unit. Young (1971) suggested calculating the coefficient of variation of the angles within the unit concerned, and comparing this with an agreed standard to give a measure of objectivity which allowed him to call this the 'best units' method. Segments and elements having thus been designated, each element is accompanied by a measure of curvature, which is the rate at which angle changes with distance down slope and is usually expressed in degrees per 100 m. The curvature of a measured length is calculated with reference to the length above and below it (Fig. 4.9). Thus, given three distances (D) and angles (A) for measured lengths a, b and c the curvature for b in degrees per 100 m will be:

$$Cb = 100 \times \frac{Aa - Ac}{2D} \quad \text{if standard distances are used, or}$$

$$Cb = 100 \times \frac{Aa - Ac}{\frac{1}{2}Da + Db + \frac{1}{2}Dc} \quad \text{if distances are variable.}$$

An example of the sort of analysis achieved by Young's method is shown in Fig. 4.10. Although more complex than simple visual classification of the profile, this approach does have the advantage that it takes into consideration not just a change in angle, but also the type of slope on which that change occurs. Thus a variability of $2°$ within a unit may be highly significant on a gentle slope but quite unimportant on a steep slope. Once the classification is complete it is possible to derive from the profile a considerable amount of statistical information, some yielded by the original survey and some calculated in the subsequent analysis. The handling of this information to provide generalised description or specific hypotheses about underlying factors is considered in the next section.

53

Slope unit	Crest segment	Convex element		Segment	Convex element	Maximum segment	Segment	Concave element		Minimum segment	Convex element	Maximum segment	Concave element	Minimum segment
Angle	0°–2°			15°		30°	25°			5°		12°		2°
Curvature		4	20		30			10	26		10		16	
		Convexity					Concavity				Convexity		Concavity	

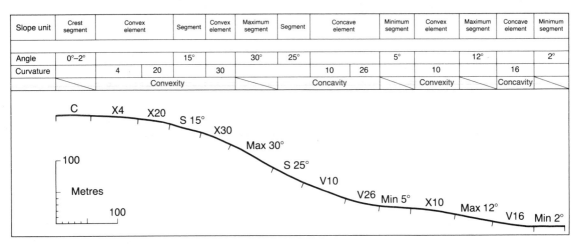

Fig. 4.10 Analysis of slope profile form (A. Young 1972).

Slope statistics

Recognising the great complexity of natural slopes, many investigations over the past century have attempted to produce and handle information in the form of slope statistics. In recent years this trend has accelerated in phase with the widespread quantification of physical geography, but two changes have become important. First, much greater attention has been paid to the sample design so as to ensure that the data are objectively representative of the whole population of slopes of a given type. Thus it has been accepted that the previous concentration on subjectively chosen 'typical' slopes had often led to the reinforcement of preconceptions rather than an open search for real patterns and variability. Secondly, greatly increased sophistication of statistical analysis has made possible the much deeper analysis of the available data, though it is noticeable that in many cases new ideas have prompted such developments in technique rather than being a product of them. Thus it is possible to extract most of the relevant information with relatively simple techniques. The increased use of statistical approaches has meant that quantitative data are no longer used largely as a basis for description, although this remains an important function. Instead, statistics may reveal patterns that suggest lines of explanatory investigation ('exploratory' uses), and provide an essential if underused means of testing the validity of hypothetical ideas about slopes, their evolution, and the reasons for their variability. Some of these possibilities can be demonstrated by a brief review of the statistics of slope angle, form and orientation.

Slope-angle statistics   These may be derived from contour maps (rapid but imprecise) or from field-surveyed profiles. They may refer to the complete range of slopes present (as in a point-sample from a map, or a compilation of all the measured lengths from a series of profiles), or may be specific indices of profiles (such as the *maximum angle* on each profile, or the *mean angle* from crest to slope-foot). A set of such values for an area can be summarised by using simple descriptive statistics such as mean, mode and standard deviation, but more information for either description or testing of difference between samples is gained by plotting frequency distributions.

A single *frequency distribution* is of limited value, but comparison between distributions can be very important, since peak frequencies suggest commonly occurring ranges of slope angle under specified conditions. Significant differences may throw light on the factors associated with slope variation. Thus Fig. 4.11 demonstrates how change may be related to rock

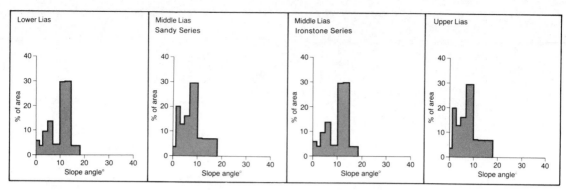

Fig. 4.11 Variations in slope-angle frequency with rock type (after K. J. Gregory and E. H. Brown 1966).

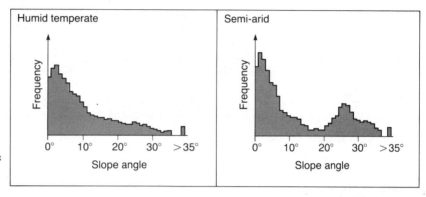

Fig. 4.12 Variation in slope-angle frequency with climatic region (after A. Young and D. M. Young 1974).

An estimation of component slope angles: Monument Valley, U.S.A. (Visual estimation is often misleading. Cliff angles are actually 65°–90°, debris slopes 30°–38° and foot-slopes 2°–8°.)

type, whilst Fig. 4.12 shows a similar degree of contrast based primarily upon climate. Humid temperate areas frequently show a single major peak frequency, usually coinciding with the relatively gentle slope angles that dominate most landscapes, though several important minor frequency peaks may be found. Semi-arid areas (such as the landscape shown in the photograph on this page) and commonly typified by a sharp contrast between

Estimation of maximum slope angles: chalk scarp near Devizes, Wiltshire, showing terracette development. (Smoothly curved profiles make estimation still more difficult. Actual maximum angles are approximately 32–34°.)

Fig. 4.13 Change of slope-angle frequency during slope evolution (after B. Finlayson and I. Statham 1980).

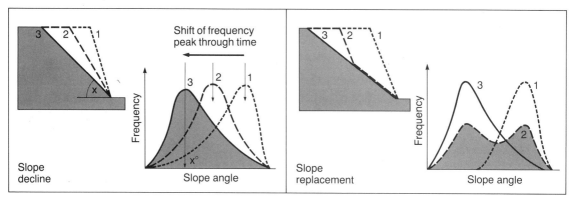

steep cliffs and gentle debris-covered foot-slopes, a pattern which appears on the frequency diagram as a bimodal distribution. It can also be shown (Fig. 4.13) that evolution of the slope though time will itself be reflected in the changing frequency distribution.

A closer analysis of the distribution of slope angles may reveal still more clues as to the factors affecting the slope. An obvious approach to investigating the processes at work is to specify the range of angles with which a particular process type is associated. The simplest version of such an approach is the designation of *limiting angles* which can be regarded as boundaries above or below which a particular process does not operate. For example, slope stability may set an upper limit to the angle at which a particular slope type may be maintained (thus the upper parts of scree slopes are often restricted to angles no greater than 36°–38°), or a lower limit to the angle needed for the operation of a certain process (thus terracettes rarely occur below 32°–33°, soil slips are rare below 20°, and rapid arctic solifluction may require slopes of at least 6°–8°).

If it is assumed that a particular combination of process and other controlling factors will encourage the production of a particular slope steepness, then the limiting angle argument can be extended to the more flexible idea of *characteristic angles*. These are narrow ranges of angles which occur with unusually high frequency either on all slopes or under particular defined conditions. Peaks on the frequency distribution graph can be interpreted as characteristic angles. Great care is necessary in the interpretation of such peaks in terms of underlying processes and factors since there may be a temptation to ascribe some fundamental explanation to something that is little more than a random local pattern. Nevertheless, the widespread recurrence of similar peaks cannot be overlooked. Young (1972) notes the particular importance of angle groupings at 45°, 33°–35°, 25°–26°, 5°–9° and 1°–4° in this context.

Slope-form statistics These are perhaps less commonly used for comparative purposes, though there is considerable potential for analysis. Profile curvature has already been mentioned as one possibility, but greater use has been made of simple classification of profiles into convex, concave and rectilinear units, followed by measurement of the proportion of the profile occupied by each form type (Fig. 6.8). The results can be used to show changes through time or from place to place, and may throw light on the reasons for these changes.

The degree of form variation is considerable. Even in humid temperate regions, rectilinear segments are more important than was realised before objective measurements were common. Such segments often lie in the steepest central portion of the profile, forming either cliffs (in areas of high relief, strong rock and active basal undercutting) or lower-angle process-controlled slopes that may well appear as characteristic angle peaks on the frequency distribution. Rapid mass movements tend to come to rest at particular angles with a given material, and slopes dominated by such processes are likely to show important rectilinear segments. Although slopes often appear rounded to the eye, it is usual for at least 10% and possibly up to 30–50% of the profile to be rectilinear (photograph p.55). Since these slopes are generally the product of effective transport processes they may be regarded as weathering-limited. Curved elements, on the other hand, evolve in response to progressive action of less effective transport which rarely exceeds the maximum rate of weathering: they are therefore usually transport-limited (p. 26).

Much argument has developed concerning the specification of links between process and curvature. It is easy to claim that such links exist, but difficult to demonstrate exactly what processes are responsible for which type and rate of curvature. Convexity has most often been attributed to soil creep, rainsplash and slope-wash, it being argued that such processes require increasingly steep slope angles down the profile in order to transport the increasing amount of material that must pass progressively lower points in a given time. Concavity is usually associated with either erosion or deposition by running water, whether as wash or as channel flow. Two common arguments are, first, that run-off increases down slope and that the consequent improvement in transporting efficiency permits transport across progressively gentler slopes and, secondly, that sediment grain size decreases down slope and thus requires ever gentler angles to induce transport. Such generalisations, however, cannot be taken too far: we have already mentioned that rockfall and talus creep produce concavity at the base of scree slopes.

Slope-orientation statistics These are of interest only in a narrow range of circumstances. In most cases the direction in which a slope faces is a product of the channel pattern, which in turn reflects local geological structure, tectonic history and sequence of geomorphological development. The interest

Fig. 4.14 Conformable and inverse slopes.

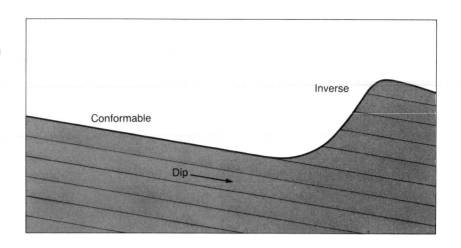

Fig. 4.15 Survey and analysis of asymmetry orientation, based on chalk slopes of the South Downs west of Eastbourne.

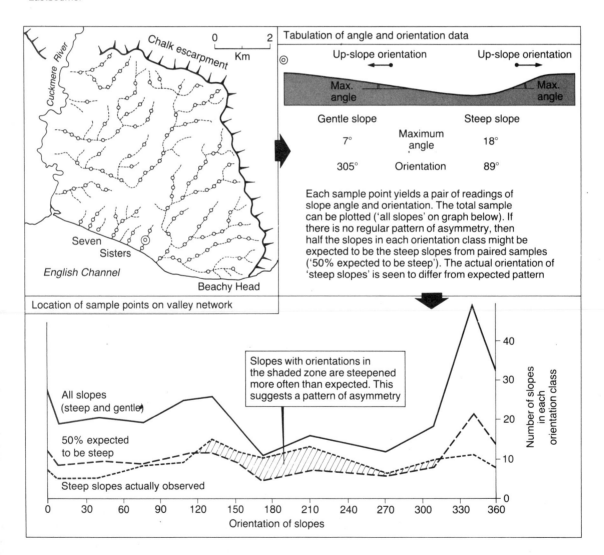

of orientation thus lies in its ability to isolate the influence of one factor from the effect of other factors – a constant problem in the analysis of multivariate relationships such as those which control slopes. Two examples will suffice. The influence of angle of rock dip on the steepness of resulting slopes was investigated by Lambert (1961). He divided slopes into *comformable* and *inverse* according to their relationship with dip (Fig. 4.14) and then tabulated the associated slope angles as follows:

Calcareous slopes	Mean slopes	
	Conformable	Inverse
Dip 30°–50°	7.4%	8.4%
Dip 50°–65°	8.0%	9.2%
Dip 65°–80°	8.6%	9.0%

This suggests that inverse slopes (such as scarp slopes) tend to be steeper and thus retreat more actively than conformable slopes (such as dip-slopes) especially with dips less than 50°. This kind of relationship is associated with both scarp retreat and the uniclinal (down-dip) migration of valleys and is discussed further in Chapter 6.

The other classic situation in which orientation has been used is in the study of asymmetrical valleys. Since these valleys have a standard geology, history and regional climate, the differences in angle of slopes facing in different directions have generally been attributed to local climate, particularly under periglacial conditions which tend to encourage differential slope development by varying snow retention, meltwater, solifluction and sediment yield to streams depending on slope orientation with respect to the sun and to prevailing snow-bearing winds. Fig. 4.15 suggests how a regional sample of paired slope profiles might provide data which can be analysed to show tendencies for certain slope orientations to be marked by particularly steep slopes. Detailed identification and interpretation of patterns of valley asymmetry are both complex and controversial, as will be seen in Chapter 7.

A framework for analysis

This brief introduction to slope form and angle has revealed a complicated and highly variable set of patterns. This information can stand in its own right as a type of landscape description, but it is more likely to be used as a basis for one of several categories of further work. Explanation is an obvious aim, and we have seen that this may be approached in a variety of ways. It can be argued that slopes reflect the relationship with underlying factors of the external environment such as geology or climate – a viewpoint explored in Chapters 6 and 7 respectively. Alternatively, it may be that the evolution of the slope is a major control of its form. This has often been claimed to be a consequence of the sequence of development which the slope has undergone, in which case the present form is dependent upon the nature of the sequence and the stage that has been reached. On the other hand, some researchers have suggested that once established, slopes retain a standard series of units throughout their life, a notion which renders the slope independent of age or stage. Since these ideas are fundamental to our understanding of slope development, they are considered in the next chapter before the detailed operation of external factors is investigated.

5 Slope evolution: observations and models

Advances in understanding are not the monopoloy of the professional scientist. In 1866 a keen amateur geologist and Sussex vicar, the Reverend Osmond Fisher, published a prophetic article on slope evolution which demonstrated clearly the problems and methods of this important topic. The fact that the outline of his findings would still be accepted today is a testimony to Mr Fisher's ability as one of the first quantitative geomorphologists, and an indication that despite great advances in detail, the underlying concepts of evolutionary thinking have changed little in over a century. We can profitably study his work as an introduction to the way in which ideas in slope evolution have developed, though it will be seen later that detailed and refined versions of the argument have been put forward more recently. Fisher observed the development of a vertical chalk quarry face. (His original diagram is reproduced as Fig. 5.1, though we shall need to refer only to a part of it.) Since the face weathers equally over its surface it remains vertical whilst retreating (CP on Fig. 5.1); and the debris accumulates at its base as a plane surface inclined at the angle of rest (PT). As the cliff retreats the debris slope extends so that the debris is spread ever more thinly over the enlarging area (RQ is larger than TP). As a consequence, the buried rock slope at the foot of the cliff becomes gentler at each stage of retreat (QP is gentler than PA, and so on) until it is reduced to the angle of rest, whereafter it is extended at that angle with a thin debris veneer until the retreating cliff is completely consumed. Fisher was able to demonstrate mathematically that the curve of the buried rock slope took the form of a parabola.

We have seen in previous chapters that minor modifications would now be made to this argument (terms such as free face and talus slope have been introduced; weathering is unlikely to be exactly equal over the whole cliff; the debris slope is unlikely to be either perfectly straight at its base, or to be inclined at the precise angle of rest of the debris), but the overall sequence remains remarkably sound. We will extend the underlying argument shortly, but first it is useful to use Fisher's hypothesis to illustrate the context within which all investigations of slope evolution have to operate.

Fig. 5.1 Facsimile of the Rev. Osmond Fisher's 1866 diagram of the retreat of a vertical chalk cliff. CP and EQ represent successive cliff positions; PT and QR represent successive debris slope positions; AP and PQ represent successive extensions of the buried rock face.

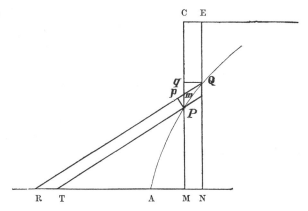

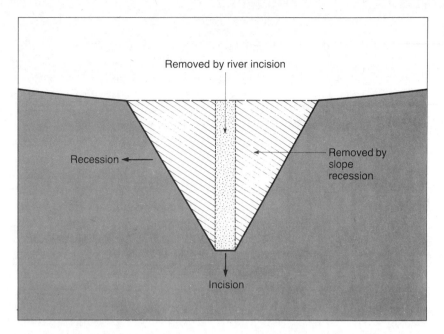

The fundamental problem is that evolution implies change of form or
position through time, but in practice the time needed is enormously greater
than that which can be covered by any direct observation. Individual slope
process events may be completed very quickly, but the impact of those few
active seconds or minutes on the overall appearance of the slope is usually
infinitesimal. We saw in Chapter 3 that Anders Rapp (1960) tabulated
a large number of mass movements in an arctic mountain valley, some of
them frequent and some involving very large amounts of material, but when
these processes are translated into their total influence on slope recession
the results are sobering:

Kärkevagge results	Minimum rock wall retreat		0.04 mm/yr
	Maximum rock wall retreat		0.15 mm/yr
Comparative results	Spitsbergen	0.02 mm/yr to	0.5 mm/yr
	Austrian Alps	0.7 mm/yr to	1.0 mm/yr

Indeed so slow is the retreat of hard rock faces that special precision instru-
ments called micro-erosion meters are needed even to detect it. At these rates
it would take between 10,000 and 100,000 years for a slope to retreat by
10 metres, and even that would have little impact on the form of a large
slope. As a consequence, almost all studies of natural slope evolution have
to use indirect methods to a greater or lesser extent.

A second source of difficulty is that it is often impossible to imagine
what the initial slope in a sequence of evolution would have been. Fisher was
helped by having the simplest possible case — a demonstrably vertical cliff
with a horizontal surface above and below. Such simplicity is rare in nature.
It is generally argued that in humid areas most initial slopes are the result
of river downcutting, whilst slope processes are entirely responsible for valley
widening (Fig. 5.2). Again, however, this is a gross over-simplification for
slope evolution purposes, since even if the river obligingly resisted all lateral
migration during its incision, we would still have to grapple with the fact
that downcutting and slope widening would take place concurrently, not
consecutively. Whilst it is possible to imagine individual cases in which convenient inital slopes might be produced (massive sudden faulting, major

volcanic event, and so on), we have to accept that this is the exception rather than the rule, and that as a result the early stages of most theories of slope evolution may be to some extent 'artificial'.

This conclusion leads us to the third general problem faced by slope evolution analysts. Specific case studies have the advantage that they can be described and tested on the basis of hard evidence, but they suffer the severe disadvantage that the resulting sequence is usually dominated by specific local circumstances (initial slope, denudation history, climate, geology). The generalisation needed to turn such specific observations into a general theory or model of slope development involves great simplification, and consequently makes it very difficult to test the resulting theory against real examples. It is interesting that back in 1866 Fisher came close to developing both a model and a rigorous verification through field data (though we have admitted that he was working with a very simple case). Since Fisher's time, slope geomorphology has experienced the trend demonstrated by many branches of science, whereby 'experimentalists' (in our case, field workers) and 'theoreticians' have followed largely separate paths. This division was very noticeable in the 1960s when detailed and quantitative study of process and form accelerated. There followed a period in which the focus on process and materials was so strong that the study of slope evolution became positively unfashionable. It is interesting that the 1980s reflect a potential reversal of this trend, leading towards a re-working and testing of old evolutionary ideas against the new data and the new understanding of process.

Given the importance of this long-term perspective, it is worth considering in more detail the several ways in which geomorphologists have approached the study of evolution. It is logical to start with direct (albeit simplified) observations, leading to indirect methods and finally to theoretical modelling.

Direct observations of slope evolution

It is very rare for investigations to be long enough, and processes active enough, for direct observation of significant slope change to be possible. For evolution to be sufficiently rapid, it is necessary for the slope to be relatively weak (easily weathered or unconsolidated) and oversteepened so that active adjustment of profile occurs. These conditions are sometimes met naturally, as in the case of undercut soft-rock coastal or river cliffs, or small fresh fault scarps. More often, investigations are directed towards artifical conditions which lead to such instability of slope that rapid response is inevitable. Fisher was just one of many researchers to work on quarry faces, one study extending to 25 years, which is almost unheard-of in geomorphology. Mining spoil tips, road or railway cuttings and embankments are other examples of popular sites for small-scale study.

An unusual case of long-term observation is under way in Southern England in association with archaeological experiments on the rate of modification of banks and ditches of the sort that were constructed by early man for defensive purposes. V. B. Proudfoot (1970) has described the geomorphological implications of an experiment at Overton Down, Wiltshire. In 1960 a ditch 27.5 m long, 3 m wide and 1.5 m deep was excavated in solid chalk, and the material used to build a tapered bank 2 m high. The development of these features and the decay of natural and artificial materials buried in them is to be monitored for 128 years, though it is acknowledged that

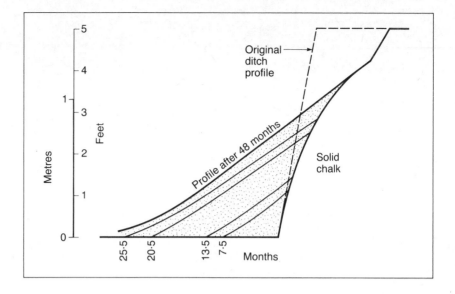

Fig. 5.3 Observed evolution of the Overton Down Experimental Slope (after V. B. Proudfoot 1970).

Experimental earthwork at Overton Down, Wiltshire.

the most marked changes will take place in the early part of this period. The walls of the ditch provide a small but valid demonstration of slope development sequence, and Proudfoot has shown (Fig. 5.3) that within 4 years the evolution of these slopes followed a pattern remarkably like that predicted by Fisher's model and later versions of it. Although the sequence is short and simple (there being no removal of debris from the slope-foot), it does show that slope development theories have some basis in reality, and that they can sometimes be tested in the field.

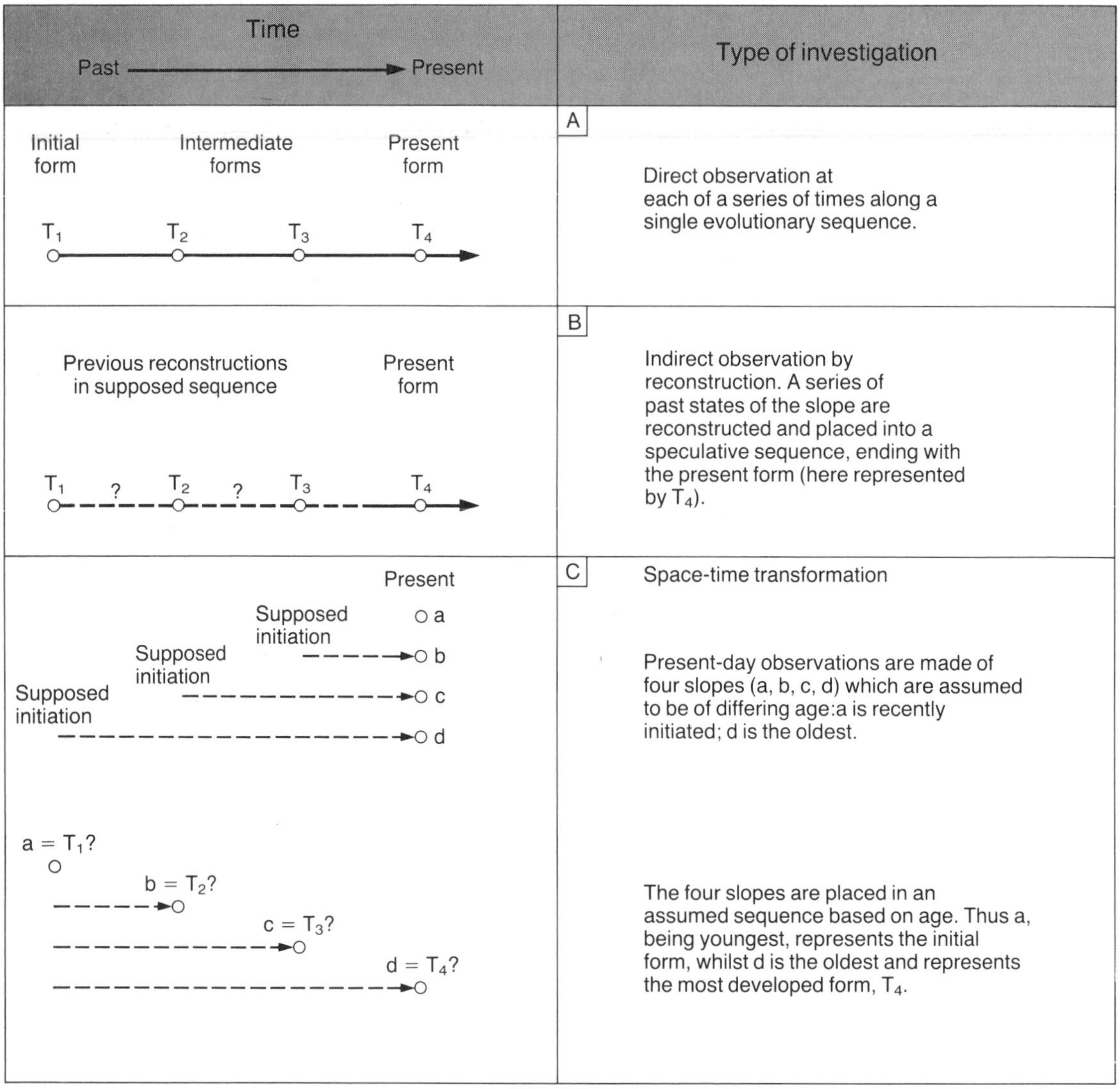

Time			Type of investigation
Past ⟶ Present			

Time Past ⟶ Present	Type of investigation
A Initial form Intermediate forms Present form T_1 T_2 T_3 T_4 ○———○———○———○⟶	**A** Direct observation at each of a series of times along a single evolutionary sequence.
B Previous reconstructions in supposed sequence Present form T_1 ? T_2 ? T_3 T_4 ○– – –○– – –○– – – –○⟶	**B** Indirect observation by reconstruction. A series of past states of the slope are reconstructed and placed into a speculative sequence, ending with the present form (here represented by T_4).
C Present Supposed initiation ○ a Supposed initiation – – – –►○ b Supposed initiation – – – – – – – – – –►○ c – – – – – – – – – – – – – – – – –►○ d $a = T_1$? ○ $b = T_2$? – – – – –►○ $c = T_3$? – – – – – – – –►○ $d = T_4$? – – – – – – – – – – – –►○	**C** Space-time transformation Present-day observations are made of four slopes (a, b, c, d) which are assumed to be of differing age: a is recently initiated; d is the oldest. The four slopes are placed in an assumed sequence based on age. Thus a, being youngest, represents the initial form, whilst d is the oldest and represents the most developed form, T_4.

Fig. 5.4 Designs for investigating slope evolution.

Indirect approaches to the study of slope evolution

Faced with the fact that the evolution of large slopes or slopes on resistant rocks takes place so slowly that direct observation is impracticable, geomorphologists have had to tackle the problem of finding an alternative approach. Many give up altogether, preferring to concentrate on the postulation of theoretical slope models which allow them to develop ideas unconstrained by the paucity of real-world data. We will look at this important branch of slope study shortly, but first it is interesting to note the ways in which a compromise has been struck between observation and speculation. Two basic approaches can be recognised.

1 Techniques of slope reconstruction

Fig. 5.4A shows in abstract form the way in which direct observation at a series of times is possible when the total time period (T1 to T4) is short. For longer time periods, a similar though less reliable sequence can be assembled (Fig. 5.4B) by reconstructing information about the state (form, angle, position) of a given slope at several points in the past. So as to place these reconstructions in the correct order, it is necessary to be able to establish the relative or absolute date of each of the time periods studied. This approach is in principle relatively easy to apply to depositional slopes, where the evidence of one time is buried and thus preserved beneath the material accumulating during the next period. Dating can then be attempted by any of the standard methods. It is clear, however, that erosional slopes (which are far more common than depositional slopes) must be reconstructed speculatively, or be approached by the second indirect method.

2 *Space-time transformation*

In those many cases where it is impossible either to observe slope evolution directly or to reconstruct it reliably using sound field evidence, the only alternative is to examine a series of different slopes in the hope of being able to argue that they represent different stages in a single sequence of evolution. This idea is depicted in Fig. 5.4C. Four slopes (a, b, c, d) are each observed at the present day. If it can be demonstrated that their development actually commenced progressively further back in time (a being the youngest and d the oldest), then their present forms can be regarded as representing stages T1 to T4 in a common sequence of development. This approach is an attractive solution to the problem of observing long-term slope time-sequences, but it is beset with difficulties. Not only does it rely on it being possible to designate the ages of the slopes concerned, but it is also essential that each of the slopes should have developed under the same conditions (the same geology, climate, altitude, tectonic and denudational history). This requirement is rarely met in practice except in relatively restricted areas, but despite this limitation we can note several creative attempts to look at changes in space and claim that they represent evolution through time. In this branch of geomorphology, imaginative investigative design is often the key to success.

On the north coast of the Solent (Hampshire, England) an 8 m cliff has developed in relatively unconsolidated sands and gravels. The construction of a breakwater at the eastern end of this cliff has encouraged beach aggradation fed by longshore drift from west to east. As a result the beach has grown wider, first of all at the eastern end and then progressively further west. This beach widening has protected the cliff from further marine undercutting (which has been responsible for keeping it oversteepened), and the cliff slope has subsequently evolved under subaerial processes. The eastern portion was the first to be protected, and has therefore been evolving longest. The western end of the cliff remains unprotected and retains its near-vertical angle. A sequence of cliff profiles from west to east (Fig. 5.5) can therefore be taken to represent a sequence of development from young to old, showing the familiar replacement of a retreating free face by an extending debris slope which ultimately reaches the cliff-top.

This sequence is based upon the idea that the removal of basal attack (wave action in the present example) initiates the subsequent development of form under the influence of slope processes. We can see the same idea in many different disguises in the literature on slopes. A closely related example is the important study by R. Savigear (1952) of slopes along the coast of Carmarthen Bay east of Pendine (South Wales) (Fig. 5.6). Within the Taf estuary to the east tidal scour has kept coastal sedimentation in check, so that steep and relatively active cliffs are found. Nearer to Pendine,

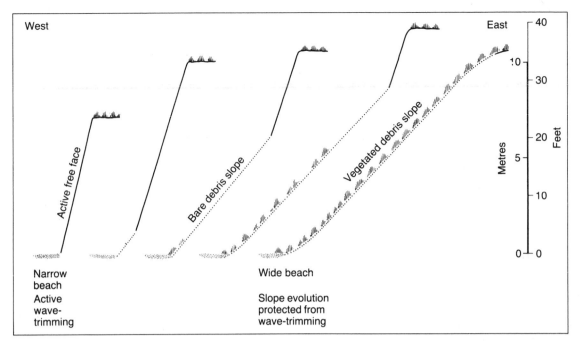

West   East

Active free face

Bare debris slope

Vegetated debris slope

Metres   Feet

Narrow beach
Active wave-trimming

Wide beach

Slope evolution protected from wave-trimming

Fig. 5.5 Form sequence in Solent cliffs.

Fig. 5.6 Evolution of marine cliffs after basal protection by marsh growth at Pendine, Wales (after R. A. G. Savigear 1952).

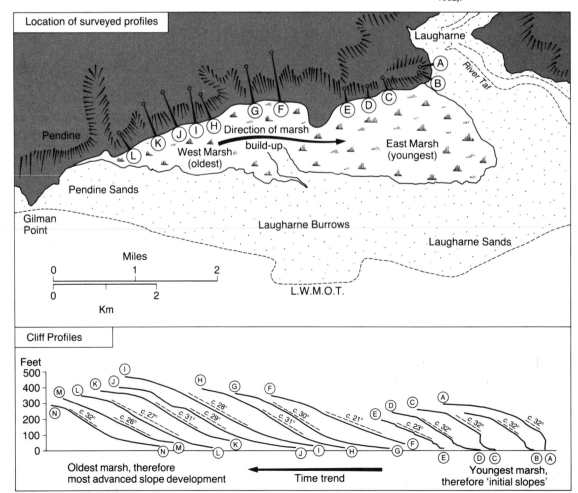

Location of surveyed profiles

Laugharne

River Taf

Pendine

Direction of marsh build-up

West Marsh (oldest)

East Marsh (youngest)

Gilman Point

Pendine Sands

Laugharne Burrows

Laugharne Sands

L.W.M.O.T.

Miles
0   1   2

0   2
Km

Cliff Profiles

Feet
500
400
300
200
100
0

c. 32° c. 26° c. 27° c. 31° c. 29° c. 28° c. 30° c. 31° c. 21° c. 23° c. 32° c. 32° c. 32° c. 32°

Oldest marsh, therefore most advanced slope development

Time trend

Youngest marsh, therefore 'initial slopes'

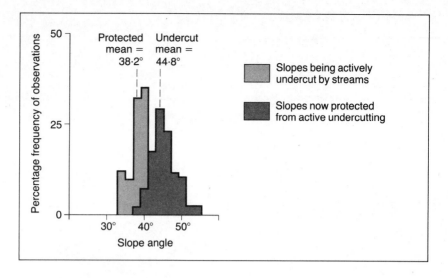

Fig. 5.7 Comparison of undercut and protected slopes in the Verdugo Hills, U.S.A. (after A. N. Strahler 1950).

however, progressive extension of marsh accumulation has protected cliffs and permitted them to develop subaerially. In this case, cliff age can be said to increase from east (where the marsh is recent) to west (where the marsh is old). Although the resulting sequence of cliff forms is less clear than in the smaller and geologically simpler Solent example, there is nevertheless an unmistakable pattern whereby the steep free face of active eastern cliffs is progressively replaced on the older western cliffs by an upper convexity, a long central rectilinear segment, and a basal concavity.

Such argument is by no means restricted to coasts. The American geologist A. N. Strahler (1950) pioneered the use of statistical analysis in slope study through an example from the Verdugo Hills, where migrating streams are actively undercutting some slopes at the present time, whilst neighbouring slopes have been abandoned by the streams and are now dominated by back-wasting. Strahler assumed that the undercut slopes were 'younger' forms from which the 'older' abandoned slopes were developing. He established a statistically significant difference between the mean angle of 44.8° for undercut zones compared with 38.2° for protected slopes (Fig. 5.7), and concluded that slope decline dominated evolution in this area. Whilst the implications of the conclusion can be questioned, the validity of the method is clear.

It would be tedious to extend the list of examples, but once the logic of the approach is understood its potential is obvious. Many other 'space-time transformations' (i.e. arguing that a sequence in space represents development through time) have been tried. Slopes above active glaciers have been compared with those recently abandoned by slope-foot ice. Volcanic islands of different ages have been investigated to see if they yield contrasting slopes, and the slope evolution following dated phases of vegetation removal has been monitored. Great efforts have been made to gather data on a seemingly intractable problem, but progress has been slow and fragmentary. Many geomorphologists over the past century have grown impatient in the face of this failure of evidence to keep up with ideas, and have turned instead to the comparative freedom of theoretical models of slope evolution.

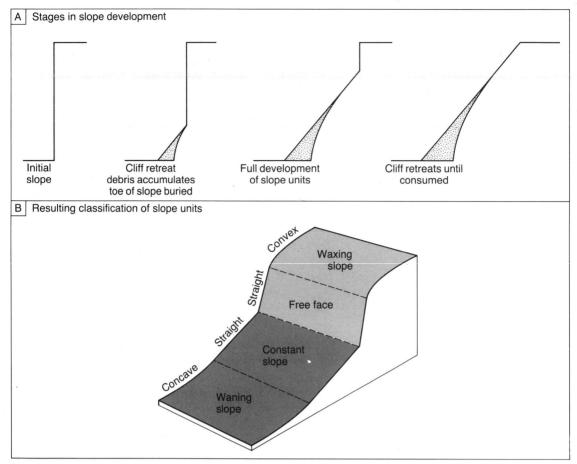

Fig. 5.8 A. Four-unit slope model, also referred to as the four-element slope profile (after A. Wood 1942).

Models of slope form and evolution

In a bid to overcome the observational difficulties of studying real slope evolution sequences, geomorphologists have made use of a wide variety of models to investigate, test and express their ideas. Laboratory and field simulations using artificial precipitation on prepared erosion plots are obvious 'physical' examples. So, too, are mathematical models which take an arbitrary initial slope and apply to it a set of numerically defined assumptions about the rate at which each portion will retreat under given conditions. This allows the calculation and plotting of a model sequence of development which can be compared with real examples in order to test the model's validity. Most so-called 'theories' of slope evolution should also be viewed in this manner. They represent conceptual models, often derived deductively from a simplified and loosely defined set of assumptions about slope change, and should strictly function as hypotheses which may be useful in the development of ideas, but have been insufficiently tested and refined to be accepted as theory. In few other branches of geomorphology have such far-reaching arguments been based on such slender evidence, and then been argued and defended with such intensity. No simple resolution of the problem seems likely in the near future, so we must be satisfied with a brief introduction to the range of available models, starting with form and then moving to evolution.

A four-unit slope profile.

Model classifications of slope form

Whilst form classification may appear to be descriptive of the present slope rather than of its evolution, the approach is relevant in that it has often been used to identify 'typical' units of the profile which are then claimed to behave in a specified manner. If the likely activity on each unit can thus be predicted, it becomes possible to argue about the probable development of the profile as a whole. So many models have been proposed that it is impossible and unhelpful to attempt a full coverage, but three examples will suffice to demonstrate the type of thinking involved. We shall find in general that as the number of subdivisions recognised by a model increases, so too does the detailed specification of form and process that can be given – but often at the expense of reducing the general applicability of the model to slopes as a whole.

The *four-unit model* proposed by A. Wood (1942) is a good example to start with, since it very clearly grows out of the sort of ideas earlier expressed by Fisher (1866). In its simplest form (Fig. 5.8A) the growth of a rectilinear talus slope beneath a retreating cliff suggests two major units, but Wood argues that particularly in humid areas an upper convexity will develop, and that weathering and further transport at the talus foot will produce a basal concavity. The resulting four units (Fig. 5.8B) he named the waxing slope (convex), free face, constant slope, and waning slope (concave). Both the model and its terminology have been widely applied in the literature over the last forty years. It has the advantage of simplicity, and by varying the proportion of the profile occupied by the standard units the model can be adapted to fit different circumstances. To develop fully, such a slope requires strong rock, a high initial slope and an absence of basal undercutting – conditions which are particularly common in semi-arid areas.

To demonstrate how this simple model can be elaborated it is worth noting two other examples. A *five-unit model* was suggested by N. Caine (1974) as being typical of mountain slopes (Fig. 5.9). This takes the same

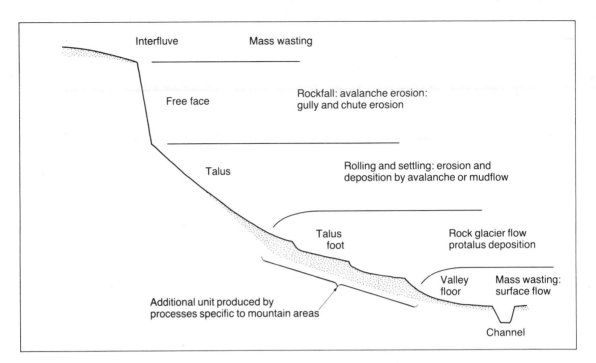

Interfluve   Mass wasting

Free face   Rockfall: avalanche erosion: gully and chute erosion

Talus   Rolling and settling: erosion and deposition by avalanche or mudflow

Talus foot   Rock glacier flow protalus deposition

Valley floor   Mass wasting: surface flow

Additional unit produced by processes specific to mountain areas

Channel

Fig. 5.9 Five-unit Alpine slope model (after N. Caine 1974).

① Interfluve
② Free face
③ Talus
④ Talus foot
⑤ Valley floor

A five-unit mountain slope profile.

basic form as the four-unit model, but adds a 'talus foot' unit between the rectilinear talus and the concave valley floor. This additional unit reflects the operation of specifically alpine periglacial processes at work in the moist mobile zone below the talus.

Once such elaboration on the basis of specific processes has been accepted, the idea can be extended to produce much more complex classifications, an example being the *nine-unit model* (Fig. 5.10) proposed by Dalrymple *et al.* (1968). Again this tends to represent a subdivision of the four-unit

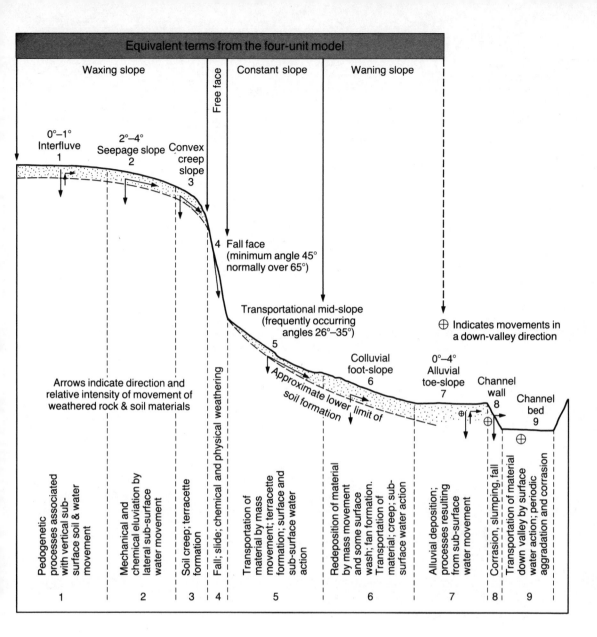

Equivalent terms from the four-unit model

Waxing slope | Free face | Constant slope | Waning slope

0°–1° Interfluve 1

2°–4° Seepage slope 2

Convex creep slope 3

4 Fall face (minimum angle 45° normally over 65°)

Transportational mid-slope (frequently occurring angles 26°–35°) 5

⊕ Indicates movements in a down-valley direction

Colluvial foot-slope 6

0°–4° Alluvial toe-slope 7

Channel wall 8

Channel bed 9

Arrows indicate direction and relative intensity of movement of weathered rock & soil materials

Approximate lower limit of soil formation

1 Pedogenetic processes associated with vertical sub-surface soil & water movement

2 Mechanical and chemical eluviation by lateral sub-surface water movement

3 Soil creep; terracette formation

4 Fall; slide; chemical and physical weathering

5 Transportation of material by mass movement; terracette formation; surface and sub-surface water action

6 Redeposition of material by mass movement and some surface wash; fan formation. Transportation of material; creep; sub-surface water action

7 Alluvial deposition; processes resulting from sub-surface water movement

8 Corrasion, slumping, fall

9 Transportation of material down valley by surface water action; periodic aggradation and corrasion

Fig. 5.10 Nine-unit slope model (after J. B. Dalrymple *et al.* 1968) with associated dominant geomorphic processes.

model, but units 7, 8 and 9 are additional. The increasing emphasis on related processes marks this as being a more recent viewpoint than Wood's rather traditional statement or Fisher's almost completely descriptive-geometrical argument. It is especially applicable to humid temperate regions, but like the other models discussed so far it relies heavily on the presence of a free face and on the simple operation of assumed links between process and form. Not surprisingly, the development of wholly general models of evolution requires even greater flexibility, and consequently introduces still more speculation.

Models of slope evolution

For largely historical reasons much of the debate about slope evolution has polarised under the ideas of two early geomorphologists, the American W. M. Davis and the German W. Penck, writing in the latter part of the nine-

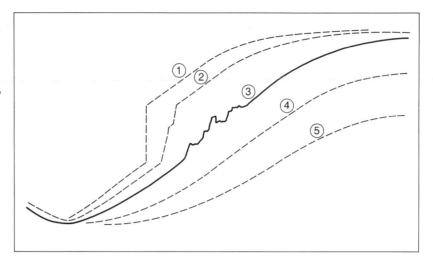

Fig. 5.11 A slope decline sequence based on the profile shown in the photograph on p.87. The profile has become graded by stage 4.

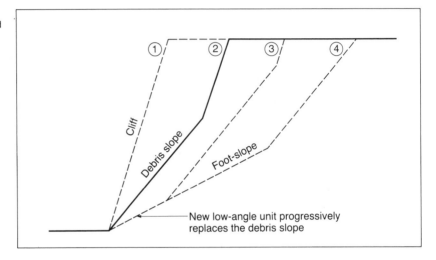

Fig. 5.12 A slope replacement sequence based on the profile shown in Fig. 5.5.

teenth century and the first part of the twentieth century. This is doubly unfortunate, both because such early ideas inevitably lacked the advantage of more recent understanding of process, and because this 'classic' phase of the debate became very confused. Davis (1899) pioneered the *slope decline* model (discussed below), and claimed that Penck supported parallel retreat – a misrepresentation which went largely unchallenged for many years since few people had read Penck in the original German version. In fact, Penck's (1924) views approximated to what we would now regard as a *slope replacement* model, whilst the third main approach (*parallel retreat*) is more closely reflected in the work of the South African geologist, L. C. King (1957). In the face of such confusion it may be acceptable to sacrifice the detail of the historical debate, and to concentrate instead on the three main models that have emerged.

(a) Slope decline After the production of steep initial slopes by a phase of rapid channel incision it is suggested that the balance between transport and weathering will induce an overall decline of the profile (Fig. 5.11). Points progressively further down the profile have to transmit not only the debris produced by weathering at that point, but also all the debris moving from

Parallel slope retreat in a semi-arid area: Monument Valley, U.S.A.

further up slope. Thus the ability of the transport processes to remove all available debris and keep the surface exposed to active weathering becomes less towards the foot of the profile. It follows that weathering, debris removal and consequent ground lowering must increase in rate up slope, leading eventually to an overall decline of the slope since its top is being lowered more rapidly than its foot. Such a sequence would be indicated in the field by the existence of central rectilinear slope segments at a variety of angles within an area of constant geology and climate. The fact that observations often reveal strong characteristic angle peak frequencies argues against the operation of simple decline in such cases. It must also be noted that decline is most likely once a smooth graded profile has been established, and is thus likely to characterise the later phases of landscape development whilst other sequences dominate the evolution of steeper slopes.

(b) Slope replacement   Several examples of the retreat of a free face above an extending debris slope have already been discussed (e.g. Fisher's chalk quarry face, the Solent and Pendine cliffs, the Wiltshire archaeological ditch). In such cases the cliff is ultimately replaced by a lower angle debris slope, though during the period of retreat it maintains its angle so that in this very limited sense there is an element of localised 'parallel' retreat (Fig. 5.12). The debris slope or talus will itself ultimately be replaced by a still gentler slope produced when the transport of increasingly weathered debris begins to extend a new depositional unit from the slope-foot. In principle this sequence can be further repeated, with each slope unit retreating until it is replaced by a lower-angle unit growing up from below. Thus although the ultimate end-product is a gentler profile, this has not been produced by the 'hinged' decline covered in the previous model. Evidence of a slope replacement sequence would be that within a given area, any specific unit such as the free face will occupy markedly different proportions of the profile, indicating its consumption by gentler units. This was, of course, the argument used to explain the Solent cliff profiles.

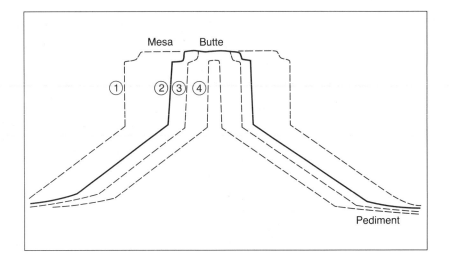

Fig. 5.13 A parallel retreat sequence based on the profile shown in the photograph on p.73.

Mesa Butte

① ② ③ ④

Pediment

(c) Parallel slop retreat In some cases, such as the semi-arid area shown in the photograph on p. 73, the free face appears to occupy much the same proportion of each profile whether it is associated with a major cliff line or a small erosional remnant (butte). This suggests that each of the upper slope units retreats by the same amount so that the whole profile (not just the individual units) retains its form but leaves an extending concave unit (a pediment) at its foot (Fig. 5.13). Only this lower unit tends to reduce in angle with time. The most likely explanation is that the development of this sequence is controlled by the rate of retreat of the free face, which in turn can be attributed to the presence of a particularly resistant rock stratum. Both geology and climate (through weathering and transport processes) thus contribute to the sequence, which reaches its optimum development in sedimentary rocks under semi-arid climate (though some authors have argued that the same model may apply in all climates).

Slope evolution in perspective

For more than half a century these competing models of slope evolution were the subject of bitter debate, but by the mid-1960s attention had begun to focus on other aspects of slope study. This trend has been helpful not so much for producing new evidence or ideas which resolved the conflict, but for allowing geomorphologists to take stock of the nature of the underlying argument. Thus although the problem still awaits solution, it is now much more clearly defined. The three models can now be unambiguously specified in theory and in the field. Carson and Kirkby (1972) have noted that in essence the discussion can be reduced to three components: (i) the *form* of the 'main slope' (the active section between the upper convexity and the lower concavity), which comprises one or more units; (ii) *internal change* of form of the main slope with time (i.e. whether or not slope replacement occurs); (iii) the *overall behaviour* of the main slope (retreat, decline, shortening, or a combination of these trends). These three attributes combine the descriptive properties of the form classifications with the evolutionary aspects of the developmental sequences, and thus offer a convenient link between the two types of model.

It is also seen as self-evident now that the three models are not mutually exclusive. All may be valid under the right conditions, and indeed a sub-

stantial proportion of the following two chapters is devoted to a consideration of the influence of rock type and climate on the nature of slope development in a given area. A final important change of outlook that took root in
the 1960s has been the general acceptance that the sequence of development
depends fundamentally on the time-scale involved. In the (geological) short
term the process thresholds that we have discussed often lead to the production of *equilibrium slopes* that retain their form through time, but are 'dynamic'
in the sense that erosion continues. Since the whole slope is lowered by the
same amount no change of form is apparent. However, such dynamic equilibrium is only likely to be long-lasting if the land is uplifted tectonically at
least as fast as its surface is being lowered by slope processes. In other cases
equilibrium will be dominant in the short term (known as 'graded time'),
whilst in the long term (known as 'cyclic time') a progressive evolution of
overall slope form is inevitable. Slopes which change in form through time
are called *time-dependent* whilst those which do not are *time-independent*.
Much remains to be achieved in the formulation and testing of evolutionary
concepts, but we shall now see that the current research priority pursues
this aim by way of the more limited focus on the influence of specific factors
on slope development.

6 Rock type and slope development

It seems self-evident that the form, steepness and evolution of slopes reflect, at least to some degree, the influence of rock type. Such a view is based partly on the fact that different rocks will be subjected to different weathering processes, resulting from variations in chemical composition, joint spacing, porosity and permeability, and partly on subjective field observations. Within Britain there are obvious comparisons to be drawn between the clay vales with their gentle and sometimes barely perceptible slopes, the chalk uplands with their rounded outlines and slopes comprising the 'ever-recurring double curve', the areas of Carboniferous Limestone where deeply cut valleys are often associated with steep craggy outcrops (free faces) and extensive accumulations of scree, and the granite moorlands of Devon and Cornwall where the mainly regular and curving slopes are interrupted in their upper sections and at their crests by the irregular outlines of the granite tors.

However, even at the outset it must be emphasised that the relationships between rock type and slope are far from simple. Lithology is only one of many factors involved in slope development, and its effects may be masked by other influences such as relative relief, valley spacing, hydrological conditions and vegetation type and cover. Although these other factors may themselves to some extent reflect geological control (for instance, a mechanically weak rock may be more deeply dissected than a hard rock, or an impermeable rock may be associated with a greater drainage density than a permeable rock), they are also profoundly affected by the 'exogenetic' control exerted by climate (Chapter 7). It is therefore unrealistic to expect a particular rock type always to produce slopes of the same form and angle; the variables involved are far too numerous. In addition it is essential to recognise that what are often regarded as 'uniform' rock types may actually contain slight but significant variations of lithology, bedding and joint spacing which, by their influence on weathering processes and mass movements, modify the course of slope development. In short, there is no such thing as a typical limestone slope, a typical sandstone slope or a typical basalt slope.

Nevertheless, it may still be possible to make some broad generalisations about the relationships between rock type and slope development. Baulig (1940), in a discussion of convexo-concave slopes, argued that the two components of such profiles are shaped by different processes, or that different processes are dominant on the two parts. He inferred that initially profiles are largely convex on rocks such as chalk and granite, which may or may not be permeable in themselves but which furnish a permeable waste cover readily transportable by soil creep but little affected by surface flow. By contrast rocks such as shales and argillites, being impermeable, are characterised by more intense surface run-off; this wash may become concentrated into rills which cut 'closely spaced furrows of very small depth, which impose a slope profile the same as their own on the crests of the low ridges between them'. Such a profile will inevitably be broadly concave. However, Baulig recognised that other factors are important. For instance, as slopes are wasted and decline in angle with the passage of time the increased accumulation of regolith on the lower part of the slope will result in more effective

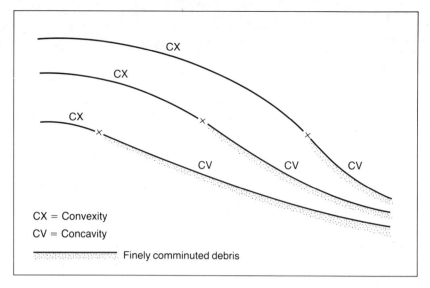

Fig. 6.1 Slope evolution (after H. Baulig 1940).

CX = Convexity
CV = Concavity

░░░░░░ Finely comminuted debris

chemical decomposition, producing in turn finer particles, greater impermeability and more efficient surface wash. Gradually the finer regolith will be extended up slope, at the expense of the thinner, coarser and more permeable layer developed there. Thus concavity will grow at the expense of convexity; and late-stage landscapes, whatever the underlying lithology, will be dominated by concave slope profiles (Fig. 6.1). Baulig's observations are in many respects over-simplified (convexity of profile may not result merely from soil creep, but may have several causes) but appear to have some validity; for instance geomorphologists have accepted that chalk (and other limestone) slopes are dominantly convex, though field study has shown that such slopes show great variability in detail.

King (1957), in his discussion of the widespread occurrence of the 'four-element hillslope' (comprising waxing slope, free face, debris slope and pediment), argues that departures from the 'ideal form' reflect the influence of bedrock rather than climate (Fig. 5.8). The most important consideration is whether lithology, with the assistance of strong relief, favours the development of the free face – in which case the other three elements are usually present. If the bedrock is strong (as in the granite-gabbro suite of rocks, quartzites and massive limestone) free faces can readily occur on high valley sides and on the flanks of prominent residual hills; if the bedrock is weak and readily weathered, free faces will be rare or non-existent, and 'degenerate, smooth convexo-concave slopes' will dominate, as in thinly bedded limestones, shales and poorly cemented sandstones. King also relates the extent of individual slope elements to lithological control. Horton (1945), in his discussion of overland flow on hillslopes, postulated a 'zone of no erosion' at the hillcrest, having a 'critical length' (x_c) from the divide over which sheet flow is so limited that its energy is insufficient to overcome soil resistivity. The critical length would vary with the intensity of rainfall, nature of vegetation cover and – relevant in the present context – infiltration capacity, which would itself be determined by the underlying rock and/or the detrital layer derived from that rock. Although we have already discussed some modification of this viewpoint, it is reasonable to suggest that in chalk and limestone country in lowland England critical length will be considerable, contributing to the very broad convexities associated with interfluve crests here (Fig. 6.2). By contrast, in areas of impermeable clay and shale in semi-arid environments, where rainfall is episodic but of high intensity and vegeta-

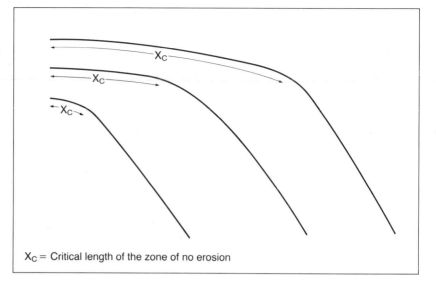

Fig. 6.2 The relationships between the critical length of the zone of no erosion and slope profiles.

X_C = Critical length of the zone of no erosion

tion cover sparse, the critical length will be minimal, producing very limited convexities and sharp-backed divides. King also emphasises that in hard, massive rocks in semi-arid areas, slow granular disintegration (for example of granite or gneiss) produces waste that is rapidly and effectively transported by wash processes operative on gentle foot-slopes; under these conditions pediments are extensively developed at the base of retreating steep scarps, and may – as in Zimbabwe – occupy up to 90% of the landscape by area.

Strahler (1950) proposes a tentative threefold classification of 'graded erosional slopes' which takes into account lithological and other influences.

(i) 'High cohesion slopes' These are developed in highly cohesive, fine-textured materials such as clays or clay-rich soil, or mechanically strong, massive bedrock such as granite, schist and gneiss. Maximum slope angles may lie within the range 40°-50° or even higher. Since such slopes exceed the angle of repose of loose dry fragments of the same material, they are generally free of debris; the latter collects at the slope base to form talus slopes of lower angle. It is important to emphasise that the formation of high-cohesion slopes requires considerable relief, the product of 'a steep gradient stream system in the process of vigorous corrasion'. For other reasons, too, the rocks mentioned do not invariably support slopes as steep as 40°-50°. Clay (and clay soil) is a porous material capable of holding considerable internal water content; as the latter increases, pore-water pressure is raised, and if the water content exceeds 50% the 'liquid limit' of the rock will be surpassed and the latter will collapse under its own weight. Similarly in very hard rocks the presence of joints and fractures, particularly where these dip down slope, will favour large-scale slope failure.

(ii) 'Repose slopes' These are developed in rocks (usually thin-bedded and/or closely jointed) which readily shed loose, coarse rock fragments. The latter mantle the slope, although being slowly removed by gravity-controlled processes. The slope itself, essentially a *denudational* form and commonly rectilinear in profile, is strongly influenced by the angle of repose of the overlying particles. With different types of rock, producing different grades of detritus, the angle of repose will vary from 25° to 40°, but is commonly

A 'repose' (boulder-controlled) slope: near Voi, Kenya.

within the range $30°$–$35°$. As with high-cohesion slopes, strong relief is a prerequisite for the formation of repose slopes. We have seen that subsequent work has suggested a distinction between repose slope and angle of rest, but the basic concept remains helpful.

(iii) 'Slopes reduced by wash and creep' These occur where, for reasons of proximity to base level or loss of stream energy, channel corrasion is reduced and channel gradients low. In these circumstances slopes cannot be maintained at their maximum angles, and are gradually wasted by sheet erosion, rain beat and creep to well below the repose angle. Such slopes (which range in angle from $1°$ to $20°$) often develop at the expense of steeper slopes by 'basal encroachment', as in the formation of pediments. Generally speaking, slopes reduced by wash and creep are independent of geological control (they appear to form on clay, sandstone, chalk and granite alike).

Morphometric studies of rock type and slope form

Early geomorphologists tended to make *qualitative* assessments of the relationships between rock type and slope form and angle (for example, the widely held belief that clay slopes are dominantly concave and limestone slopes dominantly convex). Such assumptions are clearly open to field testing by the methods of slope profile measurement and analysis. Several studies, employing morphometric techniques, have appeared since 1950, producing results that are sometimes illuminating, but often somewhat confusing.

1 *Studies of slope angle in relation to rock type*

As implied by King and Strahler, slope steepness may to a large extent reflect the influence of lithology, rock strength, bedding, jointing and the manner in which a rock weathers. Macar and Fourneau (1960) investigated the relationship between slope angle and lithology in the Charleroi region of Belgium. The basic distinction observed was between 'weak' rocks (clays, sands and chalk) and 'coherent' rocks (schists, sandstones and limestones). In the former maximum slope angles varied from $2.5°$ to $8.5°$ (mean value $5°$); in the latter from $7°$ to $33.5°$ (mean value $18°$). With regard to individual rock types there was remarkable similarity between clays and sands (mean maximum angle $5°$). Macar and Fourneau suggest that the former have been greatly reduced in gradient by periglacial solifluction, and the latter – more recently – by creep and rainwash acting on almost totally incoherent sediments. The steepest slopes (mean maximum angles 21.5 and $20.5°$) were found in sandstones and limestones; the similarity between the two is explained by the inherent resistance of the former (a function of rock strength due to compaction and cementation) and by the fact that the relative weakness of the limestone is offset by the reduced effects of rainwash, the result of high permeability.

It need hardly be emphasised that these conclusions, none of which are surprising, are of limited applicability. The noted relationships between rock type and slope angle might well need to be modified under different relief conditions (the Charleroi region is one of mainly gentle relief), in areas of different drainage density, under different climatic conditions, and so on.

As an example of slope statistical analysis we noted that the effects of structure on slopes were considered by Lambert (1961), in a study of dip on mean and maximum slope angles in limestones and psammites (sandstones) in the Condroz region of Belgium. Slopes 'conforming' with dip were, in terms of average angles, gentler than slopes 'opposing' dip (inverse slopes); such a structural situation is, of course, a commonly stated cause of valley asymmetry (Fig. 4.14). The explanation of the contrasts in steepness is presumably that where strata 'dip into' the slope, stability of the rock is inherently greater than where slope and dip are in the same direction (except in the case where dip angle exceeds slope angle, producing a greater measure of stability). Study of maximum angles revealed a more complex situation, with, in some instances, slopes conforming with dip exceeding slopes opposing dip. However, it is worth noting that, in this strongly folded area, the most gently dipping limestones (at $30°-50°$) displayed maximum angles of $11.5°$ on slopes opposing dip, compared with angles of $9°$ where slopes conformed with dip. Doubtless in areas of truly gentle dips (less than $10°$) such contrasts in slope angles will tend to be much enhanced.

A detailed study of slope angles within one type of rock, the English chalk, shows the difficulty of generalising slope–lithology relationships. Clark (1965) surveyed 114 individual chalk slope profiles in three types of location: scarp coombes, which were generally steep-sided; coastal valleys in Sussex truncated in their lower parts by cliff recession; and inland dip-slope valleys in the Marlborough Downs, Wiltshire. Maximum slope angles showed important variations between the three locations. In the coombes there was a strong peak at $29°-33°$, probably reflecting the maximum repose angle supportable by chalk undergoing weathering and transport; the overall range of maximum angles was $21°-37°$. The absence of free faces (high-cohesion slopes) is due to the fact that although chalk has the mechanical strength to support vertical faces (as on sea-cliffs), its high porosity and thus water-holding capacity renders it very susceptible to frost action, which was intense in the chalk until some 10,000 years ago; even today road cuttings in the chalk are very rapidly weathered in winter, and wire traps have to be constructed to collect the debris. In the coastal valleys, maximum angles ranged from $7°-29°$, with peaks at $19°-21°$, $13°-17°$ and $11°-12°$; in the inland valleys they ranged from $3°$ to $33°$, with peaks at $15°-17°$, $11°-12°$, $9°-10°$ and $6°-8°$. Many of these slopes thus appear to fall within Strahler's category of 'slopes reduced by wash and creep' (though solifluction would be a more accurate term in this instance). The differences in 'development' between the three sets of valleys are not easily related to variations of lithology, but are more likely to reflect valley dimensions – and in particular depth of incision. In fact, correlation coefficients between maximum angle and slope height for the subgroups were +0.53, +0.87 and +0.52. But for the inherent weakness of the chalk under conditions of periglacial weathering, the scarp coombe profiles would have been able to support free faces and debris slopes.

Since maximum slope represents the inclination of only a small part of the slope profile, it is relevant to examine the properties of other slope units. It has been observed that these may occur at certain angles (characteristic angles), which may represent the maximum inclinations at which certain processes or groups of processes occur (in which case they are also referred to as *limiting angles*). In the scarp coombes, rectilinear segments occur not only at $32°-33°$ (the maximum angle related to lithology), but at $28°$ and $26°$. Possibly the former develop where stream action has effectively removed weathered debris from the foot of the slope, and the latter where removal has been somewhat impeded. In the coastal valleys there is a very strong peak of rectilinear segments at $8°-8.5°$, the origin of which is unclear. In the inland dip-slope valleys rectilinear segments tend to occur at $6°-6.5°$ and $3°-3.5°$; many of the chalk valleys involved are strongly asymmetrical (p. 96), and the $3°-3.5°$ mode probably reflects intense periglacial solifluction acting on the gentler slopes.

It will be evident from this discussion that slope angles in the English chalk reflect a variety of influences: lithology, valley dimensions, stage of development and past climatic history.

2 *Studies of slope form in relation to rock type*

The relative importance of slope elements (convexity, concavity) and segments (rectilinearity) should, in theory, be easily determined from profiles accurately surveyed in the field (Chapter 4). Hypothetical relationships between form and rock type can then be readily tested.

Fourneau (1960), in a study of slope profiles in part of Belgium, identified five main types of slope: convexo-concave, approximately (±) convexo-concave, convexo-rectilinear-concave, approximately (±) convexo-rectilinear-concave, and complex (comprising numerous elements and/or segments). The relationships of these profiles to lithology were found to be complicated. All types of slope were developed in clays (though ± CX/R/CV were most common); 85% of slopes in sands were complex; 67% of slopes in chalk were complex, the remaining 33% being ± CX/R/CV; 85% of slopes in limestone were CX/CV; 60% of slopes in sandstone were complex, and 54% of slopes in schist were ± CX/R/CV. The contrasts between chalk and limestone, which on the basis of Baulig's arguments should form similar slopes, are especially noteworthy – though it is tempting to suppose that Fourneau's results are not typical of chalk landscapes as a whole (see below). Fourneau also noted from his study (i) that basal concavities were developed on all limestone slopes, 88% of chalk slopes, and 76% of schist slopes, and (ii) that convexities were particularly characteristic of limestones, often occupying 50% or more of the total profile length. It seems unlikely, in this area at least, that basal concavity is produced by concentrated rillwash; its wide occurrence in limestone and chalk may well be a result of past periglacial solifluction, and its rarity in sands and sandstones may reflect that fact that these are less susceptible to frost processes.

Detailed analysis of slope profiles from parts of the English chalk (Clark 1965) shows that convexo-concave (the traditionally 'normal' profile) and convexo-rectilinear-concave forms are dominant, with the latter (47% of profiles) exceeding the former (32%). Virtually all profiles have both a basal concavity and a summital convexity. The average CX/CV slope is dominated by the convexity (which occupies 63% of the total profile length) and the average CX/R/CV slope by the rectilinear segment (41% of the total profile length, compared with 37% convex). There are considerable variations according to the type of valley involved. In the deep scarp coombes, nearly all slopes are of CX/R/CV form, with the R segment occupying an average 34% of the profile and the summital convexity over 50%. In the shallower dip-slope valleys the majority of slopes are of CX/CV form; and in these the convexity (63%) is extended at the expense of the concavity (37%). Possible reasons for these variations will be considered below.

Selected studies of slope forms in different rock types

1 *Granite slopes* (Fig. 6.3)

Granite as a rock shows considerable variability, but its essential characteristics are (i) a crystalline structure, comprising quartz, feldspar, mica, hornblende and other minerals, and (ii) a well developed joint system, consisting of two or more nearly vertical joint sets which, with 'horizontal' joints, effectively divide the rock into 'cuboidal blocks'; in addition sheet joints, often curvilinear in form, develop parallel to the margins of large granitic masses. Granite is susceptible to both block and granular disintegration; in areas of intense chemical weathering the product is a thick regolith comprising large 'core-stones' in a matrix of sand and clay. Local variations in weathering reflect such factors as precise joint spacing and the coarseness of the granite (the two may be intimately related). On Dartmoor the fine-grained 'blue granite' is more rapidly attacked than the widespread coarser 'porphyritic' granite. In northern Arran there is a marked contrast between the coarse-grained granite of the east, which forms spectacular 'blocky' cliffs and spreads of gravelly detritus, and the finer-grained granite of the west, which produces a more rounded landscape and deposits of scree.

Granite outcrops are widely assumed to form spectacular domed inselbergs, tors and steep boulder-strewn scarps; in reality, whilst these forms do occur, granite also forms rather dull, undulating landscapes, blanketed by regolith.

Among the many types of granite landscape identified (Young 1972, Thomas 1976) are the following.

(a) Smoothly convex and/or concave slopes   These have developed where advanced decomposition of the granite has produced a deep regolith, comprising 'residual debris' (a structureless mass of sand and clay) with a few core-stones (Fig. 6.3A). These landscapes are developed mainly in humid regions, both tropical and temperate – though in the latter the effects of past weathering episodes, under climatic conditions both warmer and wetter than at present, may have been largely responsible for present forms.

(b) Slope profiles comprising a down-slope succession of free face, debris slope and pediment   There are marked breaks of gradient between the three components (these represent, in effect, the three main types of slope of Strahler's classification juxtaposed) (Fig. 6.3B). Such profiles are well displayed in semi-arid regions, but are sometimes also associated with moister savanna climates. The free face may take the form of a granite cliff (whose morphology in detail reflects the influence of variable joint spacing) or a curved rock outcrop ('half dome') with powerful sheet jointing. The debris slope (usually at $30°-40°$) is occupied by large boulders, derived from the free face above or by *in situ* weathering, which are being slowly reduced by granular disintegration. It is, in fact, an example of a 'boulder-controlled slope'. The pediment, concave in profile and with angles not usually exceeding $7°$, is veneered by sandy debris being transported away from the foot of the debris slope by rainwash and ephemeral streams. The evolution of such profiles, over a very long period, is likely to follow the course outlined by King in his 'cycle of pediplanation'. Parallel retreat of the free face and debris slopes will eventually consume hill-masses or reduce them to residual inselbergs and kopjes, whilst extension of pediments will result in a multi-concave landscape such as characterises wide tracts of tropical Africa.

(c) Extensive plains surmounted by steep domed hills (bornhardts) (Fig. 6.3C) King argues that such landscapes represent late-stage developments of the pediplanation cycle, but alternative explanations are possible. The plains, extensively covered by alluvium which has accumulated in shallow valley bottoms and is underlain by rotted granite (saprolite), are undoubtedly *down-wasted* by surface wash processes; these are especially effective in seasonally humid climates (such as that of the savanna) where the vegetation cover is at times sparse and fails to protect the ground surface from the impact of heavy convectional rains. The granite domes, many of which have convex profiles overall or convex summits leading down to vertical or even overhanging rock walls, may be bare of debris, though limited accumulations may mask the base of the bare granite. The precise form of the domes is related to massive curvilinear sheet joints (separating layers of rock up to 10 m or more in thickness) which result either from pressure-release mechanisms or are related to the original structures of the granite, formed by cooling, compression and tension during the process of emplacement. Such slopes can be seen as 'structural variants' of the high-cohesion type of slope. Slope recession on the margins of domes may be very slow, though undermining of the slope foot by basal sapping (a process related to the concentration of moisture in shady overhangs, along horizontal joints, or within talus accumulations) may occur in some instances. Alternatively, if the dome grows to considerable heights, as a result of prolonged 'circumdenudation', vertical joints developing parallel to the margins may initiate collapse. As Thomas (1965) has pointed out, large domes may in this way be reduced over time to 'degenerate' rocky mounds (kopjes).

(d) Rocky slopes occupied and/or surmounted by tor masses (Fig. 6.3D)
These may result under tropical conditions from the stripping away of finer decomposition products such as sand and clay, and the emergence at the surface of partially weathered, blockily jointed granite (where acidulated rainwater has begun to open up the granite joints) or the somewhat more advanced weathering layer referred to as 'the zone of core-stones with residual debris' (Ruxton and Berry 1957). Alternatively, under colder

Fig. 6.3 Slope development in different granite terrains.

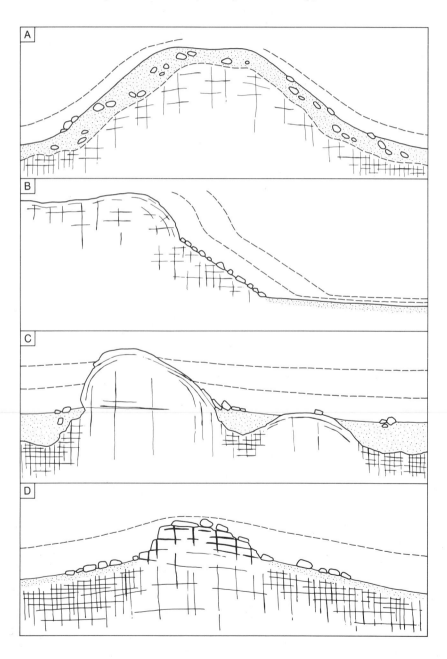

Hound Tor, Dartmoor: a summital tor showing cuboidal jointing of granite.

conditions the tors may result from differential weathering, by ice and frost action, of differentially jointed granite exposures. The resultant detritus may form blocky spreads, as in the clitters of Dartmoor.

This discussion of granite landscapes and slope forms has been far from comprehensive and has involved a high degree of generalisation. Individual granite slopes may be far more complex than those outlined. Ruxton (1958) describes a granite slope profile in the Sudan that comprises seven distinct units (Fig. 6.4). From the summit downwards this slope includes (i) a rocky cliff with large boulders, (ii) a boulder-controlled slope at $32°$, littered by 2 m boulders weathered from the cliff above, (iii) an extensive 'hill front' slope at $24°$, mantled by granitic debris, (iv) a bedrock outcrop on a slope of $20°$, (v) a slope at $13°$, mantled by weathered fragments up to 0.5 m in diameter, (vi) an upper pediment at $3°-5°$, occupied by particles up to 0.2 m in diameter, and (vii) a lower pediment at $1°$ extending downwards to a clay plain. The various component units of the profile reflect both the calibre of the granitic debris in transport and the intensity of *in situ* weathering. The 'piedmont angle' (between units v and vi) seems to coincide with the point where granite boulders disintegrate rapidly; below the angle, which is produced initially by rapid evacuation of the finer particles resulting from this disintegration, seepage water will tend to persist, intensifying chemical weathering and releasing clay particles which are washed through the subsoil to the clay plain.

2 Limestone slopes

Limestone as a rock shows greater variability than granite, in terms of chemical composition (although predominantly $CaCO_3$, many limestones have experienced dolomitisation, in the course of which the double carbonate of calcium and magnesium forms in cavities and bedding planes; 'dolomitic limestones' contain 10–40% dolomite, and 'dolomites' over 90% of the mineral dolomite), spacing of bedding planes and joints, presence of impurities such as sand, marl and silica concretions, and mechanical strength. Nevertheless, most limestones display broadly similar characteristics in relation to

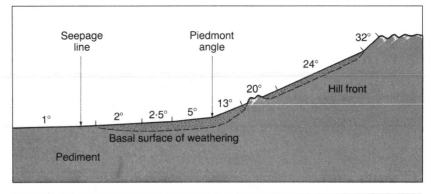

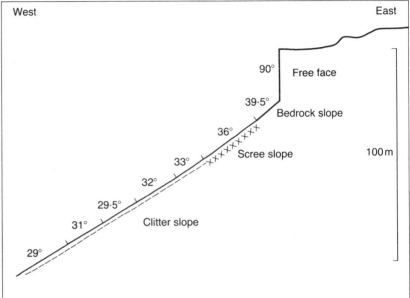

weathering: susceptibility to solution processes, which release a comparatively small amount of insoluble material, and – in cold climates – lack of resistance to frost weathering, which takes advantage of pores, joints and bedding planes to produce often massive deposits of angular detritus.

As in many other types of rock, slope forms in limestone reflect not only lithology but also relief. Deep valley incision will promote free face development, as in rocky limestone gorges, whereas gentle valleys will favour the accumulation of a continuous regolith and more rounded forms. Young (1972) states that in Britain most slopes on both hard and soft limestones are regolith-covered. 'Although sometimes appearing convexo-concave, profiling usually shows that a rectilinear segment is present; the convexity is longer than the concavity.' However, on hard limestones 'a near-vertical free face may occur, either near the crest or in mid-slope, below which occurs a 30°–35° debris slope'.

Excellent examples of the latter type of slope are seen in the Eglwyseg valley, North Wales (Tinkler 1966). Major scarp development has been promoted by the incision of the River Eglwyseg, tributary to the Dee, parallel to the western margins of the Carboniferous Limestone outcrop. Available relief here is in the order of 150 m. The area has been modified by glaciation; till is formed in places on the scarp, and gullies have been cut by meltwater. In detail the Eglwyseg escarpment shows the clear influence of rock type (Fig. 6.5). Free faces on the upper scarp face are formed by the 'White

A free face in dolomitic limestone, with debris slope in bedded limestones: Jonte Gorge, Grands Causses, southern France.

Limestone' (comprising three massive beds 8 m, 12 m and 6 m in thickness, separated by narrow shales), and beneath the free faces are bedrock slopes, scree and clitter developed on 'Lower Grey' and 'Brown Limestone' (comprising limestone bands up to 1 m in thickness, with intercalated shales in beds of up to 0.15 m in thickness). From summit to base the escarpment profile comprises up to four components: the free face, usually in excess of 50°; the bedrock slope (with a stepped form related to bedding of the Grey and Brown Limestones), with characteristic angles of 37°-39° - the latter may relate to a debris cover which has since been removed; the scree slope, formed where loose rock fragments are sufficiently deep for their dimensions and form to determine the angle of repose at 35°; the clitter slope (comprising rock fragments whose angle is determined by the angle of repose of underlying materials such as till or bedrock) at 29°-31°. In terms of slope evolution it seems likely that the major processes on the Eglwyseg escarpment have been (i) parallel retreat of the free face by mechanical weathering, and (ii) development of a buried face in bedrock, which in its upper part has been exhumed by removal of the scree cover.

More complex limestone slopes occur in the Grands Causses region of southern France. Relief is considerable, with the limestone forming plateaus at 800-1300 m above sea-level; dissection to depths of 400-600 m has been effected by rivers such as the Tarn, Jonte, Dourbie and Vis. The limestone, of Jurassic age, is lithologically varied: dolomites and dolomitic limestones alternate with strongly bedded 'lithographic' and 'sub-lithographic' limestones, and marl deposits occur at certain horizons. The *dolomites* are generally massive in character, and form major free faces on escarpments and valley sides. Since the rocks are very poorly bedded and joints are absent or wide-spaced, mechanical weathering (notably frost action) has been ineffective on these outcrops. However, in some localities surface solution has dissected the dolomite into intricate mazes of pinnacles, arches and dolines, and in extreme cases the cliffs have been transformed into isolated tor-like masses. The *bedded limestones*, by contrast, possess numerous joints and fissures, are extremely permeable, and are subjected both to sub-surface solution and surface disintegration. At present slopes in the bedded limestones are almost

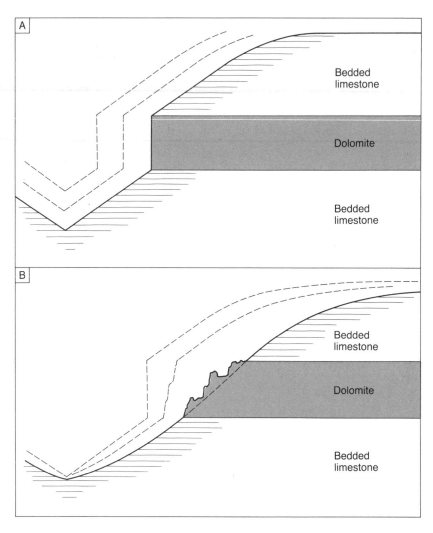

Fig. 6.6 Slope development in limestone, Grands Causses: under conditions of powerful stream downcutting (A), and no stream downcutting (B).

everywhere veneered by a regolith of subangular fragments and weathered marl; many are rectilinear, at angles of 30°–35°, and form repose slopes at the base of dolomite free faces. Where dolomite cappings are absent, convex or convexo-rectilinear slopes are formed by the bedded limestones.

In the most deeply incised valleys complex slope forms, consisting of alternate free faces and debris slopes, are developed; summital convexities frequently occur, but basal concavities form only where marls outcrop extensively at valley-floor level (Fig. 6.6A). Such stepped profiles have been regarded as typical of very youthful landscapes, with the implication that in time the free faces will be consumed by weathering and the slope as a whole will become smooth and 'graded'. However, this may be an over-simplification. The widespread occurrence in the Causses region of free faces and repose slopes in juxtaposition suggests that both can be maintained – the former by surface solution and occasional massive rock falls due to undermining at the cliff base, the latter by dominantly mechanical weathering and talus creep. Provided that relief remains considerable (as a result of continued stream incision) these profiles will be perpetuated, and rates of slope recession on the free faces and debris slopes will remain in harmony. However, under conditions of reduced downcutting and/or impeded removal of detritus from the slope base, the repose slopes will tend to decline in angle (or become

Chalk slopes near Devizes, Wiltshire.

'slopes reduced by wash and creep') and the dolomite faces to be effaced by solution and undermining (Fig. 6.6B). Stepped profiles might then gradually be replaced by 'graded' convexo-rectilinear forms. Alternatively the dolomite cliffs may be destroyed as a result of parallel retreat on either side of a divide, in which case the 'uncapped' bedded limestones will themselves weather into convexo-rectilinear or convex slope profiles.

For contrast we may turn to the slopes developed in the soft limestone chalk in lowland England. These are usually simpler in form (mainly convexo-concave or convexo-rectilinear-concave) and display no obvious effects of lithological variations within the chalk. For instance, the hard bands known as 'rocks' (the Chalk and Melbourn Rocks) separating the Upper, Middle and Lower divisions of the chalk form at best minor breaks of slope and often leave no mark at all. At present slope processes are relatively inactive, and comprise weak solution and slow creep - though on the steepest slopes the latter is sufficient to cause terracette formation. Many chalk slopes owe their form to past processes; slopes were actively steepened by meltwater streams (which were very active in scarp coombes), but wasted by rapid frost disintegration and solifluction. Aspect - and therefore susceptibility to periglacial activity - has played a major part in chalk slope development (pp. 97–98).

The manner of evolution of chalk slopes has proved singularly difficult to determine; indeed so many factors and processes have been involved that no single model seems to be applicable. Under certain periglacial conditions mass wasting seems to have produced steepening of slope angles, and under other conditions decline. Furthermore, the development of slopes in deeply cut scarp coombes (where slopes evolved during periods of rapid downcutting by meltwater) may have been different from that in shallower dip-slope valleys (where slopes may have been formed during periods of restricted downcutting or even valley-floor aggradation). From a study of down-valley profile sequences in escarpment coombes Clark (1965) has shown that initially convexo-concave slopes (the 'normal' chalk form) are converted into CX/R/CV slopes by valley downcutting, which has the effect of increasing slope height and overall steepness (Fig. 6.7). At an early 'stage' both maximum and mean slopes are less than $33°$ (the maximum repose angle for chalk slopes); as slope height increases, but the horizontal equivalent length remains constant, the central section of the CX/CV slope will steepen to $33°$.

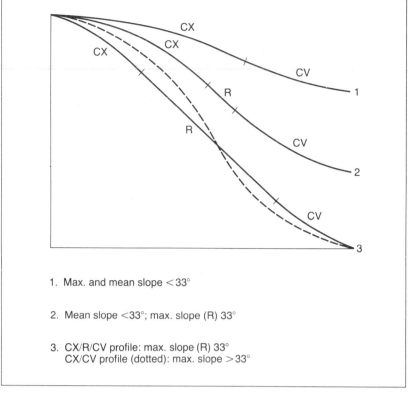

Fig. 6.7 The relationships beteem slope height, maximum repose angles and slope form in chalk (after M. J. Clark 1965).

1. Max. and mean slope $< 33°$

2. Mean slope $< 33°$; max. slope (R) $33°$

3. CX/R/CV profile: max. slope (R) $33°$
   CX/CV profile (dotted): max. slope $> 33°$

The Devil's Dyke, East Sussex: a coombe cut into the chalk scarp of the South Downs.

Thereafter the CX/CV form can be maintained only by a steepening to more than $33°$. Both theory and field evidence indicate that this is unlikely to occur, but rather that a rectilinear segment at $33°$, of steadily increasing length, will develop between the upper convexity and lower concavity. The evidence of the Devil's Dyke in East Sussex supports this model (Fig. 6.8). The rectilinearity can be seen to grow down valley, though it is a composite feature comprising segments at $29°$–$32°$ and $26°$. Very possibly the development of the rectilinearity here led to the complete destruction of the pre-existing concavity, giving a CX/R form. The present concavity is of very

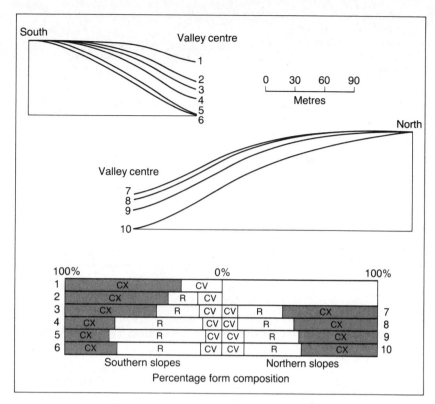

Fig. 6.8 Slope profiles of the Devil's Dyke, East Sussex (after M. J. Clark 1965).

limited dimensions (10-15% of the total slope profile in the lowest part of the Devil's Dyke), and is at least partly developed across recently formed deposits on the valley floor.

Conclusions

It is not yet possible to produce a comprehensive review of the relationships between rock type and slope angle and form. Whilst the influence of such factors as lithology, bedding and jointing on slope processes and development is manifestly considerable, it would be naive to conceive of a 'typical' slope form (or 'typical' mode of evolution) for each major rock type – just as it is unrealistic to seek 'climatically determined' slope forms (Chapter 7). There are some instances, as on granite bornhardts or the striking limestone slopes of the Causses, where rock 'control' is powerful and obvious; but there are others, as in the English chalk, where lithological influences are far more subtle. A few simple generalisations, such as that massive coherent rocks tend to produce free faces and that incoherent rocks are likely to give gentle, rounded forms, can readily be supported. However, the reservation has always to be made that the impact of rock type can be masked by other factors such as relief, climate and erosional history.

7 Climate and slope development

Climate is undoubtedly an important influence on many geomorphological processes. Frost weathering can occur only where temperatures fluctuate about 0 °C, and is therefore active in high latitudes and high mountains. Chemical weathering requires the presence of water (mainly derived from precipitation), and is speeded up by high temperatures; it therefore operates with maximum efficiency in tropical humid climates. It seems logical to suppose that if climate influences processes, and processes shape landforms, regional variations in climate will be mirrored by regional variations in types and assemblages of landforms. This is the basis of *climatic geomorphology*, the main aim of which is to identify 'morphogenetic' or 'morphoclimatic' regions; in each region, groups of climatically determined processes should produce landscapes that are in some respects distinctive. Since slopes form the major components of all landscapes, it is natural to enquire whether slope form and development reflect the influence of climate. Certainly the major processes at work on slopes – bedrock weathering and transport by running water and mass movements of the resultant detritus – are affected by changes of temperature, wetting and drying, overland flow resulting from rainfall and snow-melt, and so on.

Much of the research in climatic geomorphology has been carried out during the last two decades. However, long before this W. M. Davis had proposed his cycle of desert erosion, to account for differences of landform evolution between 'arid' and 'normal' (i.e. humid) regions. In 1942, C. A. Cotton formulated his 'cycle of savanna planation', in which he envisaged that slopes in savanna regions maintained their steepness well into the stage of old age, by contrast with the gradually declining slopes of the Davisian normal cycle. In 1950 L. C. Peltier suggested a 'cycle of periglacial erosion', in which steep frost-riven slopes were worn back by freeze–thaw weathering and replaced by low-angled pediment-like slopes over which frost debris was soliflucted into valley bottoms. Other writers, from their observations in the field, increasingly associated particular landforms with particular climatic environments, both past and present. The smoothly rounded 'mass-wasted' slope forms of the chalklands of southern England and northern France were interpreted as relict features of former periglacial conditions. Rock pediments, on the other hand, were seen as 'diagnostic' of arid environments, where they were developed at least in part by episodic water-flows (sheet-floods) at the foot of parallel-retreating 'scarps'.

However, by no means all geomorphologists have accepted that climate may play a vital role in slope development. L. C. King (1957) has argued that slopes comprise four elements (summital convexity or waxing slope; free face; debris slope; basal concavity or pediment) which occur in different combinations - though occasionally all four are present, giving a 'fully developed' slope profile (Fig. 5.8). Each individual slope element is not the result of a single process, but in different environments may be formed by different processes (e.g. convexity may be produced in a humid area by soil creep, and in a semi-arid area by rainwash). In King's view neither the slope elements singly, nor their different combinations, are climatically determined;

rather they represent the influence of lithological factors such as rock strength, jointing, calibre of weathered debris, and so on (Chapter 5).

The relationship between climate and process

Some obvious effects of climate on process have already been cited. There are many other, less obvious influences. For instance, surface rainwash – and hence erosion – is particularly active in semi-arid climates, simply because the vegetation cover is scanty (especially after a period of drought) and the rainfall infrequent but intense in character, thus encouraging infiltration excess flow. As a result the sediment loads of streams in areas receiving 250-500 mm of rain per year are exceptionally high. Even more surprising is the widespread occurrence of mudflows in deserts, owing to the prolonged collection of detritus in valley bottoms and the reduction of strength of this material by sporadic rains.

One of the earliest attempts to relate climate to process on a global scale was that of Peltier (1950), who identified nine morphogenetic regions each characterised by particular combinations of mechanical and chemical weathering, mass movement, fluvial activity and wind action (Table 7.1). However, the regions were defined in terms of only two parameters, mean annual rainfall and mean annual temperature. It is widely argued that these can provide

Table 7.1 L. C. Peltier's classification of morphogenetic regions (1950)

	Annual temp. °C	Annual rainfall (mm)	Processes
Glacial	−20 to −5	0–1100	Ice erosion Nivation Wind action
Periglacial	−15 to 0	125–1300	Mass movement Wind action Weak water action
Boreal	−10 to 5	250–1500	Moderate frost action Slight wind action Moderate water action
Maritime	5 to 20	1250–1500	Mass movement Running water
Selva	15 to 30	1400–2250	Mass movement Slight slope wash
Moderate	5 to 30	800–1500	Strong water action Mass movement Slight frost action
Savanna	10 to 30	600–1250	Running water Moderate wind action
Semi-arid	5 to 30	250–600	Strong wind action Running water
Arid	15 to 30	0–350	Strong wind action Slight water action

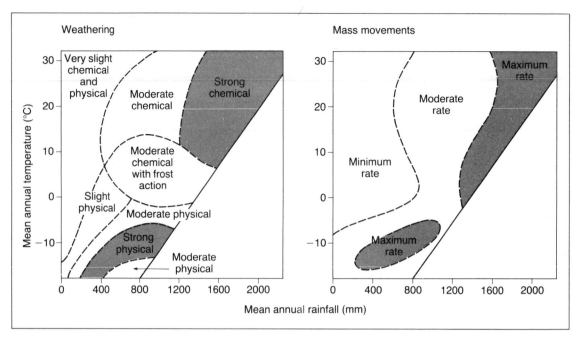

Weathering

Mass movements

Fig. 7.1 Distribution of major slope-forming processes (weathering and mass movements) with climate (temperature and rainfall) (after L. C. Peltier 1950).

at best a crude guide to process. Other writers have since sought refinement by using Thornthwaite's *P-E Index* (a calculation of *effective rainfall*, derived by subtracting evapotranspiration losses from total rainfall), data on soil microclimate, the number of days in the year with frost, and so on. Other problems arising from Peltier's approach were that (i) his statements about the role of certain processes within morphogenetic regions were intuitive rather than quantitative, and (ii) he made no attempt to relate processes to forms.

More recently, writers on climatic geomorphology have attempted the latter task, notably J. Büdel in his 1963 scheme of climatic–morphogenetic zones (Table 7.2). Of the five major zones identified (2) and (5) represent 'critical extreme cases'; both are associated with intense weathering – mechanical disintegration in the tundra 'frost-rubble' zone (2) and chemical decay in the tropics (5). Later in this chapter slope development in these two contrasted environments will be considered in detail. Peltier himself has attempted to define more precisely the influence of climate on stream activity, specifically in the context of drainage density (Dd). This in turn may be relevant to slope study, since some researchers have noted a positive correlation between Dd and slope steepness. Certainly a positive relationship between climate and

Table 7.2 J. Büdel's classification of morphogenetic regions (1973)

1 **Glaciated Zone** (polar regions and high mountains).

2 **Zone of pronounced valley formation** (in polar regions which are today unglaciated; notably underlain by permanently frozen ground).

3 **Extratropical zone of valley formation** (most of the mid-latitude regions). Valley-forming processes are of little importance today, but fossil features of glacial periods are usually much in evidence.

4 **Subtropical zone of pediment and valley formation.**

5 **Tropical zone of planation surface formation.**

Note: 2 and 5 represent the 'extreme critical cases' – both are associated with 'deep weathering' of different kinds: 2 is the tundra 'frost rubble' zone, and 5 is the zone of intense chemical weathering.

drainage is to be expected, though it will not be the obvious one of increased rainfall causing increased Dd. Other factors are important, notably the type and intensity of precipitation and the nature of the vegetation cover (thick forest may reduce Dd by favouring enhanced evapotranspiration and percolation). Gregory (1976) has noted that highest values of Dd occur in semi-arid areas or areas with a markedly seasonal precipitation regime, such as savanna or Mediterranean climates. In humid mid-latitude areas Dd is lower, though there is increase in line with mean annual precipitation within the zone. In humid tropical areas Dd values are usually greater than those of the humid temperate zone. However, another factor controlling surface flow, and therefore Dd, is relief (steeper slopes promote greater overland flow); hence any attempt to relate Dd to climate must also include reference to the relief factor.

Peltier's own observations, made from topographical maps and therefore reliant on the accuracy of those maps, were aimed to give a world-wide picture of Dd. For each area studied both mean slope and the 'number of drainage-ways per mile' were noted, and the data plotted graphically. The resultant 'curves' seemed to show the possibility of real areal differences, notably betweeen 'fluvial', 'tropical' and 'glacial moraine' landscapes.

Other approaches to the study of climate and process have centred on attempts to measure rates of denudation. Again there are clear implications for slope development, since the sediment loads of rivers – on which the calculations of denudation are normally based – are derived largely from weathering and transportational processes currently active on those slopes. Data on sediment yield are not always readily available. From a relatively small sample (of 78 basins) Fournier (1960) found that (i) seasonality of rainfall is a major factor increasing 'erosion', and (ii) relief is a powerful 'masking' factor (within a particular climate, sediment yield in mountain areas can be very much greater than from the lowlands). Highest values of sediment yield were derived from tropical regions, notably parts of W. Africa, India and Malaysia (in excess of 2000 tonnes of sediment per square kilo-metre per year), and lowest from deserts such as the Sahara, Arabian and Australian (less than 10 tonnes per square kilometre per year). In terms of the effects upon morphology, including slopes, there are unfortunately serious problems of interpretation. For one thing, the present pattern of 'erosion' may have little bearing on existing landforms, many of which may be relict – as in deserts, where many striking slope forms persist owing to the absence of present-day erosional activity. For another, the present pattern of sediment yields may reflect the impact of man, who by removing vegetation and under-taking intensive and often unwise cultivation has greatly accelerated erosion rates. Douglas (1969) has found that sediment loads in tropical rivers are often surprisingly low, with concentrations below 100 mg per litre even in flood conditions. A peak of 1,609 mg per litre in the headwaters of the Sungei Gombak, Malaysia, resulted almost entirely from erosion of a new road cut-ting during an intense storm.

Climate, slope transport and slope angle

It is often assumed that particular transportational processes are dominant in particular morphogenetic regions. Thus soil creep is associated with humid temperate slopes, solifluction with periglacial environments, rainwash with pediments in arid and semi-arid areas, and large-scale earth slips and mudflows with humid tropical landscapes. Certainly the impact of climatic elements on transportational processes is easy to discern. Soil creep, the slow down-slope movement of superficial soil or rock debris, may be due primarily to heaving and settling of individual particles, induced either by freeze–thaw or cyclic moisture changes due to infiltration and evaporation of rainwater. Gelifluction, a more complex flow process involving reduction in friction between particles caused by increased pore-water pressure as the permafrost partially melts in summer, is undoubtedly conditioned by seasonal and diurnal changes of temperature. Writing of mass movements as a whole Carson (1976) states that infiltration of water into the regolith, either during rainstorms or periods of snow melting, more than any other factor acts as the trigger for rapid movements, owing to (i) the increased bulk weight of the regolith, producing increased shear stresses, and (ii) even more important, the formation of 'perched water bodies', an increase of pore-water pressures, and reduced friction along potential shear planes (in other words, reduced shear strengths).

The quantity of soil moisture present is then a vital factor determining the efficiency of mass transport on slopes, and also the maximum angles that slopes can support. It has been shown, by Strahler (1950) among others, that within small areas maximum slope angles deviate only slightly from the mean. The maximum angles developed are not fortuitous, but are related to the 'threshold angle' of the regolith; hence the term 'debris-controlled slope'. The threshold angle normally approximates to the angle of repose of the particles comprising the regolith – though in reality, owing to slight disturbances of various kinds (frost, wetting, biotic influences) a very slow but steady creep of regolith particles down slope occurs. Carson (1976) argues that threshold slope angles ought to show a close association with climate for two reasons. First, where little wetting of the regolith is effected, stability is inherently greater owing to the high degree of friction between individual particles. Such *frictional slopes*, with a relatively steep angle, are most characteristic of arid climates. Secondly, where regolith particles are periodically wetted stability is reduced (except in the case of coarse rock rubble and talus where friction remains high). Such *semi-frictional slopes*, with a relatively gentle angle, are most characteristic of humid climates.

The implication that in arid climates slopes more readily retain their steepness (or experience parallel retreat), whilst in humid climates slopes gradually lose steepness (or undergo decline), is in line with observations of contrasts in form between desert and humid temperate slopes. However, such easy generalisations need to be treated with caution. First, frictional threshold slopes have been noted in deeply weathered granite in Hong Kong (a seasonally wet area, with an annual precipitation of 2100 mm) and other tropical humid regions, owing to the presence of an oxidised crust impeding percolation into the regolith. Secondly, a comparison of slopes developed in clay-shales in southern Ontario and Derbyshire (which are similar in amount and distribution of annual precipitation) has shown that the former are frictional (at $25°-30°$) and the latter semi-frictional (at $4°-14°$). The differing hydrological conditions in the two areas are seemingly not a function of climate, but reflect slight geological differences which cause groundwater levels in Ontario to lie well below the ground surface (in fact, at depths of 15–30 m).

An invaluable pioneer study of possible relationships between climate and slope steepness was that of Melton (1957), who undertook measurements in 80 drainage basins in Arizona, Colorado, New Mexico and Utah. Parameters of basin form included in Melton's analysis were (i) maximum valley-side slopes (ii) drainage density and (iii) relative relief (vertical distance between interfluve crests and valley floors). The most useful climatic parameter was taken to be Thornthwaite's P-E Index (see above). The basins were divided into four subgroups according to geological characteristics, and statistical correlations made between slope angle and relative relief, slope angle and drainage density, and slope angle and P-E Index. The relationships that emerged were complex and often difficult to interpret. In general, greater relative relief was, as expected, associated with steeper slopes, though not in basins developed in limestone, sandstone and quartzite. Increased Dd was also positively correlated with slope steepness, particularly in granitic areas (again an expectable result); but the two parameters were inversely correlated in the basins underlain by limestone, sandstone and quartzite. A positive correlation between P-E Index and slope angle was noted for granite (as P-E rose from 40 to 474 slope angles increased by $4°$); but a negative correlation was found in low relief sandstone, limestone and shale basins (as P-E rose from 12.8 to 77 slope angles were reduced by $5.5°$).

The most obvious conclusion to be drawn from Melton's study is that simple associations between climate and slope do not exist. However, on reflection it will be seen that climate can have indirect effects on both drainage density (which tends to be reduced as P-E increases) and depth of valley incision (by streams which are dependent on precipitation). The problem is, of course, that both Dd and relief are also influenced by non-climatic factors such as rock type, structure and erosional history. This leads us to emphasise, once again, that landforms result from the interplay of endogenous (geological) and exogenous (climatic) factors; and that it is therefore dangerous to attempt explanations of landforms, and in particular such complex features as slopes, in terms of climatic influences alone. Nonetheless, it is still helpful to isolate climatic controls of slope development, since in areas of 'identical' rock type and relief slope variations may occur that can be attributed only to climate.

Selected studies of slope forms in different climates

1 *Slope development in periglacial environments*
  (the 'frost-rubble' zone of Büdel)

That slope form and evolution can be profoundly influenced, at least by 'microclimate', in periglacial environments can be readily demonstrated. Clatford Bottom, a S.E.-trending dry valley in the Marlborough Downs of Wiltshire, is strongly asymmetrical. Its N.E.-facing slopes attain maximum angles of $20°$–$24°$, while the opposing S.W.-facing slopes are mainly at $3°$–$5°$. Excavations have revealed that the valley floor and gentler valley side are occupied by a layer of coombe rock (up to 3–5 m in thickness), formed by frost shattering and solifual transport of the highly susceptible chalk. By contrast, the steep valley side is veneered by a thin 'modern' soil. The inference must be that the gentler slope was highly 'active' under past periglacial conditions (which prevailed in this area until some 10,000 years ago); at the same time the steep slope must have remained relatively 'inactive'. It seems likely that the present asymmetrical valley was produced from a formerly more symmetrical valley by a combination of (i) periglacial mass wasting, leading to decline of slope steepness, on the S.W.-facing slopes, and (ii)

Clatford Bottom, Marlborough Downs, Wiltshire: a strongly asymmetrical chalk valley.

Fig. 7.2 Suggested stages in the evolution of valley asymmetry, Clatford Bottom, Wiltshire.

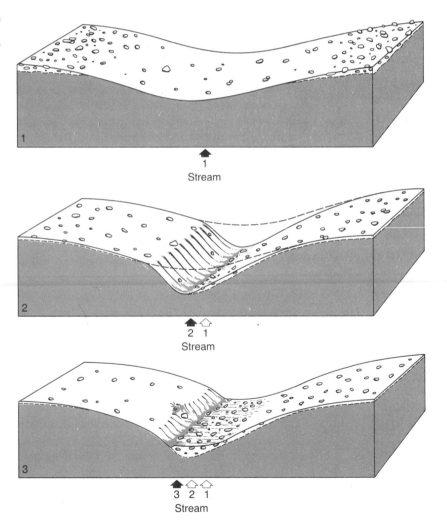

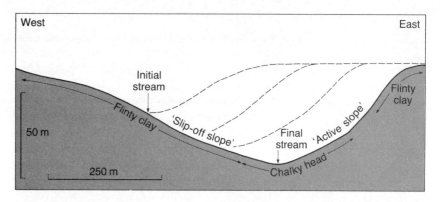

Fig. 7.3 Periglacial development and present cross-section, Little Hampden Valley, Chiltern Hills (after C. D. Ollier and A. J. Thomasson 1957).

An asymmetrical valley in a periglacial area showing snow accumulation on the gentle slope: western Canadian Arctic.

basal undercutting of the steep N.E.-facing slope by a contemporary melt-water stream, literally pushed south-westwards by the large quantities of solifluction debris (including many large blocks of silicified sandstone, or sarsens) arriving at the valley floor (Fig. 7.2).

This example shows that aspect, producing different 'microclimates' on opposing valley sides (relating to different inputs of solar energy, exposure to prevailing winds, and contrasts in snow accumulation), can influence slope modification in periglacial environments. In Clatford Bottom the factor of solar radiation may have been pre-eminent (producing more effective thawing of S.W.-facing slopes during the daytime, and thus increased frost shattering and gelifluction), though predominantly south-westerly winds may also have banked up, by the lee effect, considerable snow thicknesses against N.E.-facing slopes – though a problem here is that snow is not always 'protective' but may act as a source of moisture that aids both gelifraction and gelifluction.

Whether insolation or wind direction (or both) are involved, effects such as those observed at Clatford Bottom should occur on a regional as well as a local scale. Of course, the other factors leading to valley asymmetry (such as gently dipping rock structures, contrasting lithologies on opposing valley sides, and crustal warping) need to be discounted if 'climatic control' of asymmetry is to be safely identified. In Europe many early studies of relict periglacial valleys revealed the prevalence of steeper S. and S.W.-facing slopes. Ollier and Thomasson (1957) noted in the Chiltern Hills (i) that S.W.-facing slopes were noticeably steeper in certain large dip-slope valleys, (ii) that the steeper slopes were mantled by chalky head deposits transported by a 'process of turbulent creep' or solifluction, and (iii) that under periglacial conditions the active slopes had been actively steepened, rather than being reduced as at Clatford Bottom (Fig. 7.3). Evidently the assumption that, in periglacial environments, mass wasting leads to slope decline is altogether too simple. In fact, it has become increasingly realised that in relict periglacial areas of Europe both N.- and N.E.- and also S.- and S.W.-facing 'asymmetry' occurs. Tricart has related the development of the two types to variations in the periglacial climate. When this was relatively 'warm', owing to a greater maritime influence, S.- and S.W.-facing slopes were steepened. However, under 'cold' continental conditions N.- and N.E.-facing slopes became steeper. The complexity of the problem is emphasised by the fact that in parts of North America asymmetry is well developed only in E.-W. trending valleys (with the steep slopes consistently facing to the north). Here the insolation factor, rather than wind direction, is evidently pre-eminent (Kennedy 1976).

From this brief discussion of periglacial asymmetrical valleys it will be seen that slope development in this type of environment is a very complicated process. This is further underlined by French (1976), who argues that solifluction does not dominate slope evolution in the way that is commonly assumed. The role of slope-wash, for instance, has been seriously underestimated; on some unvegetated slopes, especially in the more arid and semi-arid parts of the High Arctic, it may exceed solifluction in its transporting capacity. The process of nivation (combining frost shattering, gelifluction and slope-wash) is also locally important, and contributes to the evolution of both 'macro' slope forms (nivation cirques and hollows) and 'micro' forms (cryoplanation or 'altiplanation' terraces).

French argues that there is no one slope form or assemblage which may be regarded as unique to the periglacial environment or 'distinctly periglacial in nature'. The following slope form assemblages are all common in periglacial regions.

(a) The 'free face and debris slope' profile   Examples of this occur in parts of Spitzbergen. It is produced mainly by gelifraction of cliffs inherited from glacially steepened valley walls (Fig. 7.4A). At the base of the debris slope, a 'zone of solifluction' (at an angle of $10°-25°$) and a gentle 'wash-slope' (at $2°-5°$) may extend the profile.

(b) Smooth debris-mantled slopes   These comprise convexo-concave elements with a continuous layer of frost-shattered solifluction debris (Fig. 7.4B). They occur in present-day periglacial environments such as Spitzbergen, the western High Arctic and Banks Island, N. Canada, and also as relict forms in humid temperate areas such as southern England and northern France. In some localities, the upper slopes are interrupted by valley-side tors, resulting from differential down-wasting or the selective destruction of former free faces (as in parts of the Pennines and Dartmoor).

(c) Basal concave slopes (cryopediments)   These are developed at the base of steeper valley slopes (Fig. 7.4C). Characterised by gentle gradients, shallow concavity of profile, and a foot-slope location, these forms seem broadly analogous to the pediments noted from tropical and subtropical regions. Like

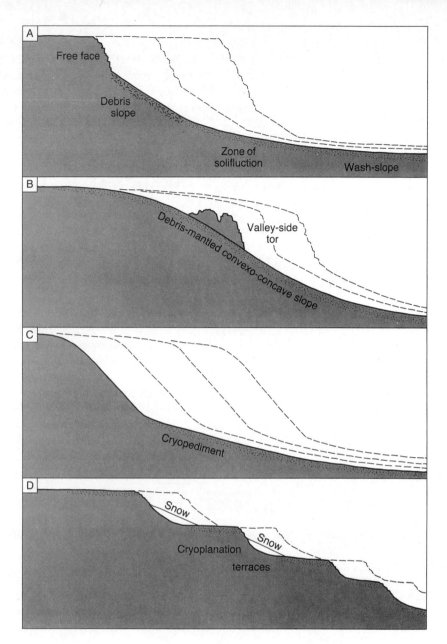

Fig. 7.4 Slope development in periglacial environments.

pediments, they are veneered by superficial debris in transport by slope-wash, aided by solifluction, from the main valley-side slopes, which are 'eroded back' by frost action and rillwash. In eastern Siberia cryopediments sometimes extend for 3 km at the base of interfluves, and may link adjacent valleys to give 'pediment passes'. The cycle of slope evolution seems to operate much as in semi-arid tropical regions, with 'slope replacement' the principal mechanism. This involves scree slopes replacing cliffs by retreat and headward extension, and in turn low-angled concave slopes replacing scree slopes. This slope replacement model may be particularly applicable to the more arid periglacial environments.

(d) Cryoplanation terraces and stepped profiles   These, far from being 'graded' with overlying sheets of solifluction debris, show a greater or lesser degree of irregularity (Fig. 7.4D). The latter may in part result from localised accumulations of soliflual material, in the shape of solifluction terraces with 'risers' up to 2–3 m high. More strikingly, in some areas there are numerous gently inclined benches, separated by bedrock outcrops or bluffs; the hill-top surface itself may be remarkably flat. Such profiles are evidently due to parallel recession of the bluffs as a result of nivation and frost action; the intervening terraces are rock-cut surfaces veneered by debris transported by solifluction and sheet-wash. The occurrence of snow-banks and snow-patches at the rear of the 'treads' is a pre-requisite for formation, but the snow must not accumulate to the extent of becoming protective of the underlying rock; thus terrace profiles of this nature develop most effectively in continental periglacial climates of moderate aridity.

2 *Slope development in tropical environments (Büdel's 'Tropical zone of planation surface formation')*

It is often presumed that the processes of landform development, including slope evolution, operate differently in tropical areas from the way they act in other morphogenetic regions. For one thing, chemical weathering in humid and sub-humid zones of the tropics is more efficient than elsewhere. The resultant deep regoliths, sometimes exceeding 60 m in thickness, are such that it can be assumed that rock waste is produced more rapidly than it is removed. Büdel points to the occurrence in tropical terrains of major escarpments separated by extensive plains; the former are relatively unbroken by the effects of stream erosion, and the latter are slowly lowered by sheet-wash processes which transfer alluvium to broad zones of accumulation on shallow valley floors. Another factor is that highly distinctive landforms are developed in the tropics, notably 'hills of circumdenudation' that range from massive monolithic inselbergs to 'castellated' tors and kopjes. At least in part these erosion residuals represent exposed and modified 'domes' on the basal surface of weathering. The stripping of the latter is effected mainly by down-wasting of the overlying regolith, following regional uplift and/or reduction of vegetation cover by climatic change.

However, as in the case of periglacial landscapes, generalisations about tropical landforms must be made with care. For example, King (1948) states that back-wearing of hillslopes, allied to extension of pediments, is the dominant process in tropical semi-arid environments. The activity of surface running water is extremely efficient, so much so that the finer products of weathering are rapidly transported away, permitting optimum development of four-element slope profiles (pp. 68–69), particularly in massive rocks which weather relatively slowly in this climate. Back-wearing and pedimentation can also affect deeply weathered areas, especially where the surface layers have been indurated to give extensive lateritic ironstones (ferricretes). Where the latter are breached by streams, valleys are formed and widened rapidly within the incoherent sands and clays beneath the laterite; the latter functions as a cap-rock, which is undermined by removal of subjacent regolith (Fig. 7.5). Although the laterite 'breaks away' to litter the slopes with fragments, it effectively strengthens the crest of the slope, causing it to maintain steepness of angle as it retreats. As the valleys within the regolith are broadened, gentle wash-slopes (pediments) extend at the foot of the parallel-retreating faces.

Although this whole process of slope formation and retreat is in a sense geologically determined, the effects of climate are also important. The process of deep weathering, responsible for the existence of the regolith, is most

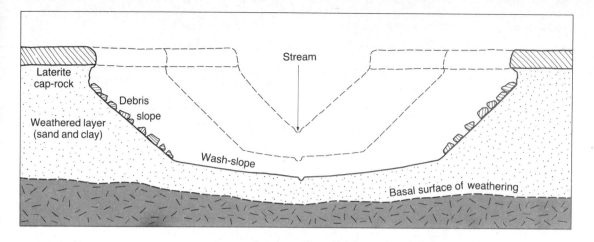

Fig. 7.5 Slope development
in deeply weathered terrain
with lateritic ironstones.

characteristic of tropical humid conditions; the formation of duricrusts
requires a strongly seasonal climate; and the dissection of the regolith may
be initiated by a change to climatic aridity, which destroys vegetation and
promotes episodic but powerful surface run-off and erosion. De Swardt
(1964) argues that 'multicycle landscapes' in tropical Africa, comprising
dissected sheets of 'older' and 'younger' laterites and associated regoliths,
represent the effects of successive climatic changes, during the Tertiary,
from humid to arid and vice versa.

Many observations have been made of hillslope form and development in
'transitional' (savanna) regions, with their distinct alternating rainy and hot
dry seasons. A dominant element here is, yet again, the low-angled pediment
slope – indeed pediments form the greater part of the landscape within existing savanna regions, although traditionally researchers have associated them
with more arid landscapes. As in drier regions, savanna pediments are concave
in profile, and are separated by a sharp break of slope (knick) from the steep
scarp. Surface wash, transporting fine debris, is usually the dominant process,
though under a relatively dense vegetation cover in southern Uganda 'lubri-
cated creep', affecting small grains of broken-down laterite, is said to operate
on pediments.

The scarps in savanna environments vary in scale from low laterite-capped
bluffs to massive, complex features such as that described by Thomas (1974)
on the western flanks of the Jos Plateau, Nigeria (Fig. 7.6). In its upper part
this scarp comprises a laterite capping, overlying *in situ* weathered material
and volcanic and alluvial sediments. This upper zone is being eroded back to
expose an inselberg-and-tor landscape which is at present being affected by
renewed weathering and transportational processes. Below this there is a
steep escarpment, with many exfoliating domes, which drops 200 m to a
series of coalescent alluvial fans. Such a complicated slope has clearly been
produced by varied processes, though Thomas argues that downcutting of the
adjacent plain and allied growth of the escarpment has been more important
than back-wearing (parallel retreat), which has affected only the uppermost
section of the scarp.

Separating scarps and pediments in savanna regions there may be depressions (linear or marginal depressions), which either run parallel to the scarp
foot or extend away from it, or both. One suggestion is that the scarp-foot
zone is subject to intense chemical rotting (related to overlying water-bearing
talus or the presence of groundwater close to the surface); this can be etched
out by springs extending headwards along lines of weakness crossing the
pediment.

103

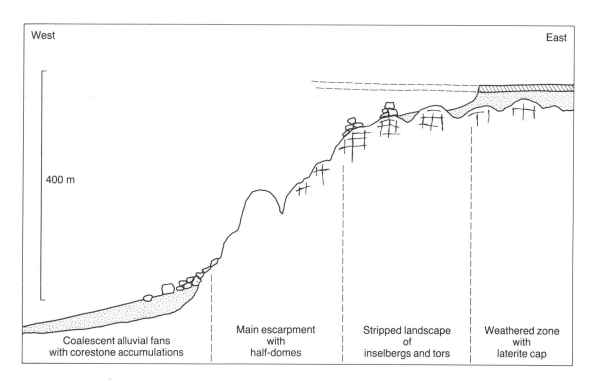

West   East

400 m

| Coalescent alluvial fans with corestone accumulations | Main escarpment with half-domes | Stripped landscape of inselbergs and tors | Weathered zone with laterite cap |

Fig. 7.6 Major granite scarp, western Jos Plateau, Nigeria (based on M. F. Thomas 1974).

Evidently the cycle of pediplanation, as envisaged by King, requires some modification if it is to be applied to the distinctive landforms of the savanna. Whereas in arid areas pediments are 'rock-cut' surfaces, in savanna areas they usually transect deeply weathered layers (in some instances it is not clear whether the pediment post-dates the weathering, or vice versa). There are important distinctions, too, to be drawn between the savanna and the more humid tropical zone. Whereas in the former residual granite hills are frequently in the form of bare rock domes (bornhardts), strongly convex in profile and occasionally with vertical or overhanging margins from which weathered material has been removed, in West Malaysia such hills are mantled by weathering profiles that extend from foot-slope to summit – indeed in many instances regolith persists on slopes in excess of 30°, owing to the protective and anchoring mantle of vegetation and the reduced effects of surface run-off. Furthermore, in the humid tropics pediments, though widely developed, are always deeply weathered and often pass upwards into the hillslope without the intervention of a basal knick. In Johore, Malaysia, the main slope elements are (i) the hillslope at 10°–40°, (ii) pediment at 1°–9°, and (iii) the clay plain; the profile as a whole seems to represent a modified form of the savanna and arid slope sequences. However, in some humid areas the pediment may actually be dissected to depths of up to 150 m, by contrast with the shallow ephemeral channels of the arid rock pediment, and a new suite of slope elements thereby initiated.

Büdel has suggested that the essential contrasts between the arid and humid tropics may be stated as follows: in arid areas there is active slope retreat, and passive extension of valley floors and plains via pedimentation; in humid areas the plains are formed by active weathering, which continually leads to undercutting of passive hillslopes. If such a distinction is valid – and the evidence presented suggests that there really are important variations in slope development within tropical environments – it seems safe to suppose that this is primarily the result of climatic controls over weathering, mass transport and run-off.

Conclusions

Climate, acting through its control of weathering, mass transport and running water, undoubtedly has an influence on the form, steepness and development of slopes. However, the precise relationships between climate and slopes are difficult to define for several reasons. There is certainly no one slope form characteristic of each morphogenetic region; rather, all kinds of hillslope are to be found in all types of climatic regime. For example, pediments seem to occur as widely in periglacial regions as in arid, savanna and tropical humid regions. Within any morphogenetic region there is no one suite of distinctive processes. Certain individual processes operate in most morphogenetic regions, though with varying intensity; and within these regions there are variations in the efficiency of particular processes (see the contrast between the importance of surface wash processes in humid and arid periglacial environments). Nor can it be confidently stated that a particular mechanism of slope evolution (parallel retreat) is characteristic of some climatic regions, and another (slope decline) of different climates.

The causes of the complexity of the relationships between climate and slopes are that (i) many present slopes are 'relict', having been fashioned under past climatic conditions; (ii) in such instances slope forms are not in equilibrium with currently acting processes – indeed the processes may be determined by the form, rather than vice versa; (iii) the 'natural' slope system has been modified by man's activities, so that measurement of active processes may lead to false inferences about slope formation; and (iv) – most important of all – it has to be recognised that climate is one of several factors in slope development (the others include rock type, structure, rate of uplift, erosional history, hydrological conditions, relief, drainage density and vegetation). The fact that some of these other 'controls' are themselves partially determined by climate renders the problem even more difficult.

8 Applied aspects of slope geomorphology

It is relatively easy to show that there is a significant relationship between man and slopes. The many processes of mass movement and slope erosion have a direct impact on our use of land, and can also in extreme cases pose a major threat to life and property. At the same time it is clear that human impact on natural slopes now represents a major factor affecting process, form and evolution both deliberately and inadvertently, whilst the production of completely artificial slopes (cuttings, embankments, spoil heaps, quarries, dams) is locally important. However, the existence of such relationships does not in itself establish applied slope geomorphology as a viable proposition. Application of a science can be claimed only if it can be shown that the skills and understanding developed by that science have actually been used to solve a real-world problem or enhance a real-world development. At this very practical level it is more difficult to make out a case for applied slope geomorphology, not because such application is absent or uncommon, but because it is so often combined with or submerged beneath other skills and other disciplines.

The relationship between geomorphology and engineering is particularly important in this context, not least because in practical terms engineers have a long-standing domination of the professional investigation of those site attributes that might be regarded as relevant to slopes. During the past decade geomorphologists and engineers have started to move rather closer together both in interest and in professional co-operation.

The value of this improved co-operation lies in the blend of skills and scales that it makes possible, and there is certainly no implication that the two approaches could or should be fused. The engineer focuses on the properties and behaviour of materials when subject to specified forces, and in order to apply his techniques widely assumes whenever possible the operation of standard relationships. The geomorphologist tends to concentrate on a wider view of the environmental content of a particular site, and is particularly interested in deducing (or predicting) process and material characteristics from the interpretation of often subtle properties of slope form. Geomorphology is often more accurate in defining the variables operating in a given location, but less precise in specifying the nature or response of any particular variable.

The difficulty of separating slope geomorphology from engineering geology or civil engineering is exacerbated by the problem of isolating the slope-related component within an applied professional study that almost always covers a broad range of topics. At the risk of over-simplifying the field, however, it is perhaps valid to recognise four elements in the application of slope geomorphology, with the proviso that these often appear in combination and that indeed a single analysis or diagram may well serve several functions at once.

Land-use potential and resource location

To recognise that slopes influence the use that can be made of land and the resources that can be found at a particular location is an exercise in pure academic geography. To map and use slope information as a practical means of finding resources and planning land use is, on the other hand, a clear example of applied slope geomorphology. In some cases slope-angle maps have been used with the class boundaries chosen to reflect information relevant to a single clearly defined property such as stability of surface material or development of soil. More often slope is just one of the attributes being mapped (that is to say, it is incorporated within a more general morphological or geomorphological map), and the aim is to define areas of relevance to a range of land-use considerations. This multivariate approach has broad applicability, but tends to be imprecise since there is no one scale of slope values that is relevant to all land-use decisions. Planners may be interested in designating 'good' and 'bad' areas for development, but the influence of slope takes place in so many ways that even the most crude analysis of relationships quickly reveals contradictory trends:

Type of slope influence	Slope angle category		
	Gentle	Moderate	Steep
Microclimate	Poor ◄---	GOOD ---►	Poor
Erosion/soil-loss (water)	LEAST	----------------►	Worst
Erosion/soil-loss (wind)	Worst ◄---	LEAST ---►	Moderate
Ground stability	GOOD	----------------►	Poor
Ground drainage	Worst ◄----------------		BEST
Flood inundation risk	Worst ◄----------------		LEAST
Aesthetic appeal	Low ◄----	HIGH	

In order to improve on this rather confusing intuitive assessment, many attempts have been made to specify precise land-use limits in terms of slope angle, usually by quoting those angles which function as the upper limit for a particular use. Although the classifications suggested vary somewhat, an underlying pattern of agreement emerges as long as it is acknowledged that an element of variability is inevitably introduced by local factors such as climate and geology.

Although still open to refinement, this kind of listing clearly offers considerable scope for turning a slope-angle map into a valuable planning document, especially in areas where the existing level of development and the available maps and surveys are both relatively limited. The major potential is, therefore, in the less developed countries of the world. Even in this context it is sometimes found worthwhile to map slope as such, particularly for very large intensive developments; but more usually the extensive area involved makes it more appropriate to include slope as just one type of information within a general survey. For practical purposes rather than for academic interest, several related techniques have appeared since about 1950 under the general heading of 'terrain classification' or 'land evaluation' (Ollier 1977). Common to all these approaches is the idea that any landscape can be divided and subdivided into ever smaller units, most of which will be repeated across the landscape. These units are defined in terms of many factors (including

Slope Angle	Land-use limitation
$0°30'$	Few obstacles to land use except poor drainage and flood risk. Limit for international airport runways.
$1°$	Mainline railways and large motor vehicles affected. Limit for local airport runways. Beyond this angle some influence felt on large-scale agriculture. Flood risk still present.
$2°$	Ideally the maximum for major roads and railways. Large-scale agricultural machinery and irrigation hindered. Some influence on building development. Flood risk replaced by threat of soil erosion.
$4°$	Development of housing and roads difficult.
$5°$	Real problems for large-scale mechanised agriculture. Contour farming advisable. Maximum for railways and for large-scale industry.
$8°$	Limit for large-scale site development. Problems for wheeled tractors and combine harvesters.
$12°$	Limit for industrial and housing construction.
$15°$	Road building difficult. Absolute limit for wheeled vehicles including tractors. Ploughing impossible without contour terraces.
$25°$	Mostly forestry and pasture land. Transport possible only with special vehicles.
$35°$	Extreme limit for caterpillar vehicles. No possibility of agriculture or building. Even forestry now limited by difficulty of mechanised extraction.
$55°$	No further economic utilisation apart from mountaineering, though land still 'useful', for example as water catchment or for aesthetic appeal.

slope, as well as landform, geology, soil, vegetation and drainage), and show an excellent correlation with economic activity or potential. Thus a map of terrain units can serve as an effective indication of the land-use potential of an area.

Hazard avoidance and prediction

One of the most horrifying aspects of major slope disasters such as the Saint-Jean-Vianney clay flow or the Huascarán debris avalanche is that there appeared to be no warning. However, the liquefaction threat of the sensitive clays around Saint-Jean-Vianney was well known, the whole village was known to have been sited with the scar of a much larger 400–500-year-old slide, and 8 days before the 4 May catastrophe a smaller slide had occurred on the banks of the Petit Bras (Fig. 3.1) at the very spot where the main slide was thought to have commenced. In the case of the Huascarán avalanche, too, though there was no local warning of the actual triggering earthquake, the avalanche hazard was certainly known. A similar avalanche in 1962 had half destroyed the village of Ranrahirca (Fig. 3.12), but it had been rebuilt on the same site. It took a second disaster to make the point that this particular area had an unacceptably high risk.

Hazard mapping and prediction thus offer a real possibility of reducing the cost and death-toll from active slope processes. In contrast to the rather mechanical mapping of slope angle as an index of land-use limitation, hazard zoning requires an understanding of the process, familiarity with the field and

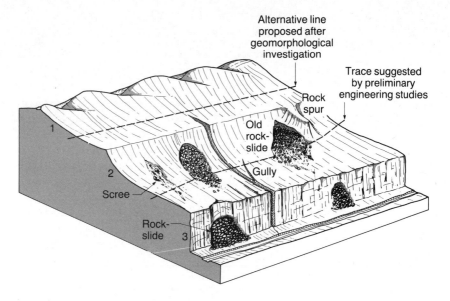

Fig. 8.1 Land units on route of Dharan–Dhankuta road, showing preliminary and revised road locations (after D. Brunsden *et al.* 1975).

aerial photographic appearance of both recent and old examples of the process, and a keen awareness of the environmental factors likely to cause it. Consequently this task requires much greater geomorphological skill.

A most convincing demonstration of the potential of geomorphological investigation to reduce slope hazard is given by D. Brunsden *et al.* (1975) in the context of a civil engineering project to build a road between the Himalayan towns of Dharan and Dhankuta in Nepal. Although only 18 km apart, these towns were separated by exceptionally rugged terrain, much of which showed three slope components (Fig. 8.1). The lower gorge slopes above actively incising rivers were extremely precipitous and for the most part impossible to cross. The mid-slopes were still steep, and gave every indication of fresh and fossil scree slopes and landslide scars – yet this was the location proposed for the road by the preliminary development brief. Only the upper slopes were relatively gentle and stable. In order to reduce costs, a major part of the site investigation was based on geomorphological survey rather than standard engineering techniques. The results demonstrated clearly that process dynamism on the mid-slopes would rule out road construction and maintenance, and established that it would be preferable in the long run to plan the road to gain height quickly in a series of hairpin bends up relatively stable stretches of the valley side, and then keep to the stable upper slopes wherever possible, thus largely avoiding the high-risk mid-slopes that had previously been designated for the route.

Environmental impact evaluation

Whilst most of the examples just quoted refer to natural hazards, the occurrence of which may possibly be related to inadvertent human action, there are many cases where deliberate and planned developments are likely to impinge upon slope processes. In such cases it is preferable to evaluate the nature and intensity of this potential environmental impact before implementing the development. An awareness of impact can then be used to decide whether or not the development is worthwhile, to adjust the development so as to minimise impact, and to facilitate the design of any necessary protective or remedial action. In the U.S.A. an *Environmental Impact Statement* must

109

be prepared as part of the statutory procedure for gaining planning permission for major development projects. In other countries the use of such an approach is less formalised. Elements of impact assessment may be included in a more wide-ranging survey, as was the case in the Dharan–Dhankuta road project which involved consideration of the likely effect of road-building on the already very unstable ground of the mid-slopes. Prediction of future change needs either a great deal of objective information about the relationships that have applied in other similar situations, or it relies upon a detailed understanding of how the processes actually work. Thus the great research effort on topics such as rainfall simulation on slopes, the behaviour of stones moving onto and across screes, the relationship between vegetation and surface flow or sediment yield, and the detailed mechanism of soil through-flow all have a great practical as well as academic interest

Slope management and control

The final category in this brief survey of types of application is the most advanced and direct – actually using a knowledge of slope geomorphology to control the processes at work on a slope rather than just predicting or locating and then avoiding the problem. Foundation instability and mass movement represent major difficulties in the use of many slopes, both natural and artificial. 'Management' can certainly be aided by geomorphological understanding, since many of the triggers of instability can be identified by the geomorphological approach. Once these factors have been specified action can be taken to hold their operation in check. However, it is doubtful whether geomorphology as such has a direct contribution to make to this control stage in the modification of process. The stability analysis of the engineering geologist together with the soil-mechanics approach and construction-design ability of the civil engineer would seem to place this stage of the work firmly within the bounds of engineering rather than geomorphology. Nevertheless, we have seen enough to appreciate that the advances made by slope geomorphologists over the last few decades have not only added greatly to our understanding of this vital component of the environment, but have also moulded the subject into a form which affords great practical as well as academic potential.

References

Baulig, H. (1940) Le profil d'équilibre des versants. *Annls. Géogr.* **49**, 81–97.

Brunsden, D., Doornkamp, J. C., Fookes, P. G., Jones, D. K. C. and Kelly, J. M. H. (1975) Large-scale geomorphological mapping and highway engineering design. *Quart. J. Engineering Geol.* **8**, 227–53.

Büdel, J. (1963) Klima-genetische geomorphologie. *Geogr. Rundschau* **7**, 269–86.

Caine, N. (1974) The geomorphic processes of the Alpine environment. In J. D. Ives and R. G. Barry (eds.) *Arctic and alpine environments,* 721–48.

Carson, M. A. (1976) Mass wasting, slope development and climate. In E. Derbyshire (ed.) *Geomorphology and climate*, 101–36. London.

(1979) Slopes and slope process. *Progress in Phys. Geogr.* **3**, 132–40.

Carson, M. A. and Kirkby, M. J. (1972) *Hillslope form and process.* Cambridge.

Chambers, M. J. (1966) Investigations of patterned ground at Signy Island, South Orkney Islands. *Brit. Antarct. Surv. Bull.* **9**, 21–40.

Chorley, R. J. and Kennedy, B. A. (1971) *Physical geography: a systems approach.* London.

Clark, M. J. (1965) The form of chalk slopes. *Southampton Res. Ser. in Geogr.* **2**, 3–34.

Cooke, R. U. and Doornkamp, J. C. (1974) *Geomorphology in environmental management.* Oxford.

Cooke, R. U. and Warren, A. (1973) *Geomorphology in deserts.* London.

Cotton, C. A. (1942) *Climatic accidents in landscape making.* Christchurch, New Zealand.

Dalrymple, J. B., Blong, R. J. and Conacher, A. J. (1968) A hypothetical nine-unit land-surface model. *Zeit. Geomorph.* **12**, 60–76.

Davis, W. M. (1899) The geographical cycle. *Geogrl J.* **14**, 481–504.

Demek, J. (1972) (ed.) *Manual of detailed geomorphological mapping.* I. G. U. Commission on Geomorphological Survey and Mapping. Prague.

De Swardt, A. M. J. (1964) Lateritisation and landscape development in parts of Equatorial Africa. *Zeit. Geomorph.* **8**, 313–33.

Douglas, I. (1969) The efficiency of humid tropical denudation systems. *Trans. Inst. Brit. Geogr.* **46**, 1–16.

Finlayson, B. and Statham, I. (1980) *Hillslope analysis.* London.

Fisher, O. (1866) On the disintegration of a chalk cliff. *Geol. Mag.* **3**, 354–6.

Fourneau, R. (1960) Contribution à l'étude des versants dans le sud de la Moyenne Belgique et le nord de l'Entre-Sambre-et-Meuse. *Ann. Soc. Géol. de Belg.* **84**, 123–51.

Fournier, M. F. (1960) *Climat et erosion.* Paris.

French, H. M. (1975) Man-induced thermokarst, Sachs Harbour Airstrip, Banks Island, Northwest Territories. *Canadian. J. Earth Sci.* **12**, 132–44.

(1976) *The Periglacial environment.* London.

Gregory, K. J. (1976) Drainage networks and climate. In E. Derbyshire (ed.) *Geomorphology and climate*, 289–315. London.

Gregory, K. J. and Brown, E. H. (1966) Data processing and the study of land form. *Zeit. Geomorph.* **10**, 237–63.

Griggs, D. (1936) The factor of fatigue in rock exfoliation. *J. Geol.* **44**, 783–96.

Horton, R. E. (1945) Erosional development of streams and their drainage basins: hydrophysical approach to quantitative morphology, *Bull. Geol. Soc. Amer.* **56**, 275–370.

Kennedy, B. A. (1976) Valley-side slopes and climate. In E. Derbyshire (ed.) *Geomorphology and climate*, 171–201. London.

King, L. C. (1948) A theory of bornhardts. *Geogrl J.* **112**, 83–7.

(1957) The uniformitarian nature of hillslopes. *Trans. Edinb. Geol. Soc.* **17**, 81–102.

Lambert, J. M. (1961) Contribution a l'étude des pentes du Condroz. *Ann. Soc. Géol. de Belg.* **84**, 241–50.

Lewin, J. (1966) *A geomorphological study of slope profiles in the New Forest.* Unpubl. Ph. D. thesis, University of Southampton.

Macar, P. and Fourneau, R. (1960) Relations entre versants et nature du substratum en Belgique. *Zeit. Geomorph.* Suppl. 1, 124–28.

Melton, M. A. (1957) An analysis of the relation among elements of climate, surface properties and geomorphology. Office of Naval Research Project NR 389–442, Tech. Rep. No. 11. Columbia University, New York.

Ollier, C. D. (1969) *Weathering.* Edinburgh.

(1977) Terrain classification: methods, applications and principles. In J. R. Hails (ed.) *Applied geomorphology*, 277–316. Amsterdam.

Ollier, C. D. and Thomasson, A. J. (1957) Asymmetrical valleys in the Chiltern Hills. *Georgl J.* **123**, 71–80.

Peltier, L. C. (1950) The geographic cycle in periglacial regions as it is related to climatic geomorphology. *Ann. Ass. Amer. Geogr.* **40**, 214–36.

Penck, W. (1924) *Die morphologische analyse.* Stuttgart.

Proudfoot, V. B. (1970) Some recent field and laboratory experiments in geomorphology.

In Studies in Geographical Methods, *Geographia Polonica* 18, 213-26.
Rapp, A. (1960) Recent development of mountain slopes in Kärkevagge and surroundings, northern Scandinavia. *Geogr. Annaler* 42, 65-200.
Ruxton, B. P. (1958) Weathering and sub-surface erosion in granite at the Pridmont Angle, Balos, Sudan. *Geol. Mag.* 95, 353-77.
Ruxton, B. P. and Berry, L. (1957) Weathering of granite and associated erosional features in Hong Kong. *Bull. Geol. Soc. Amer.* 68, 1263-92.
(1961) Weathering profiles and geomorphic position on granite in two tropical regions. *Revue Géomorph. Dyn.* 12, 16-31.
Savigear, R. A. G. (1952) Some observations on slope development in South Wales. *Trans. Inst. Brit. Geogr.* 18, 31-51.
(1965) A technique of morphological mapping. *Ann. Ass. Amer. Geogr.* 55, 514-38.
Strahler, A. N. (1950) Equilibrium theory of erosional slopes, approached by frequency distribution analysis. *Amer. J. Sci.* 248, 673-96 and 800-14.
Sugden, D. E. (1968) The selectivity of glacial erosion in the Cairngorm Mountains, Scotland. *Trans. Inst. Brit. Geogr.* 45, 79-92.
Tavenas, F., Chagnon, J.-Y. and La Rochelle, P. (1971) The Saint-Jean-Vianney landslide: observations and eyewitnesses' accounts. *Canadian Geotech. J.* 8, 463-78.
Thomas, M. F. (1965) Some aspects of the geomorphology of domes and tors in Nigeria. *Zeit. Geomorph.* 9, 63-81.
(1974) *Tropical geomorphology*. London.
(1976) Criteria for the recognition of climatically induced variations in granite landforms. In E. Derbyshire (ed.) *Geomorphology and climate*, 411-45. London.
Tinkler, K. J. (1966) Slope profiles and scree in the Eglwyseg Valley, North Wales. *Georgl J.* 132, 379-85.
Tuckfield, C. G. (1969) Relict landslips in the New Forest, Hampshire. *Proc. Hants. Field Club for 1968* 25, 5-18.
(1973) Seepage steps in the New Forest, Hampshire, England. *Water Resources Res.* 9, 367-77.
Washburn, A. L. (1967) Instrumental observations of mass-wasting in the Mesters Vig district, N. E. Greenland. *Meddelelser om Grønland* 166 (4), 1-296 (Discussed also in his book *Geocryology,* 1980.)
Wood, A. (1942) The development of hillside slopes. *Proc. Geol. Ass.* 53, 128-40.
Young, A. (1971) Slope profile analysis: the system of best units. In *Slopes: form and process.* Inst. Brit. Geogr. Spec. Publ. 3, 3-13.
(1972) *Slopes.* Edinburgh.
(1974) *Slope profile survey.* British Geomorphological Res. Group Tech. Bull. 11. Geo Abstracts, Norwich.
Young, A. and Young, D. M. (1974) *Slope development*. London.

Suggestions for further study

Specialist texts on slopes are available at a variety of academic levels for those who wish to follow up the ideas introduced in this book. These include:
Young, A. and Young, D. M. (1974) *Slope development* (Macmillan Education, London). A 35-page introduction to slopes and slope study suitable for sixth-form students and for introductory purposes.
Finlayson, B. and Statham, I. (1980) *Hillslope analysis* (Butterworth, London). This can be used with profit by sixth-form students, but is particularly appropriate as an introduction to process, material and the 'engineering approach' for first- or second-year students in Higher Education.
Young, A. (1972) *Slopes* (Edinburgh). An advanced text for undergraduate use.
Carson, M. A. and Kirkby, M. J. (1972) *Hillslope form and process* (Cambridge University Press, Cambridge). An advanced text for undergraduate use.
An audio-visual introduction to the study of slopes of particular interest to sixth-form students and those taking general courses on physical geography or environmental science is:
Clark, M. J. and Allen, W. J. (1981) *Slope - the key to landscape* (Rank Audio-Visual. Colour; 18 minutes; sound; 16 mm).
A concise aid to field study of slope profiles for advanced students is:
Young, A. (1974) *Slope profile survey*. British Geomorphological Research Group Technical Bulletin no. 11. Published by Geo Abstracts Ltd., University of East Anglia.